W9-BMG-046

SILAS MARNER

THE GREENHAVEN PRESS
Literary Companion
TO BRITISH LITERATURE

READINGS ON

SILAS MARNER

Barbara A. Goodman, *Book Editor*

David L. Bender, *Publisher*
Bruno Leone, *Executive Editor*
Bonnie Szumski, *Series Editor*

Greenhaven Press, Inc., San Diego, CA

Every effort has been made to trace the owners of copyrighted material. The articles in this volume may have been edited for content, length, and/or reading level. The titles have been changed to enhance the editorial purpose. Those interested in locating the original source will find the complete citation on the first page of each article.

Library of Congress Cataloging-in-Publication Data

Readings on Silas Marner / Barbara A. Goodman, book editor.
    p.   cm. — (The Greenhaven Press literary companion to British literature.)
    Includes bibliographical references and index.
    ISBN 0-7377-0358-X (lib. bdg. : alk. paper). — ISBN 0-7377-0357-1 (pbk. : alk. paper)
    1. Eliot, George, 1819–1880. Silas Marner. I. Title: Silas Marner. II. Goodman, Barbara A. III. Series.
    PR4670 .R36   2000
    823'.8—dc21   99-055867
                                                                        CIP

Cover photo: Stock Montage, Inc.

Copyright ©2000 by Greenhaven Press, Inc.
PO Box 289009
San Diego, CA 92198-9009
Printed in the U.S.A.

" *To a certain extent, I think* Silas Marner *holds a higher place than any of the author's works. It is more nearly a masterpiece; it has more of that simple, rounded, consummate aspect, that absence of loose ends and gaping issues, which marks a classical work.* "

—Henry James, *Atlantic Monthly*, 1866

CONTENTS

Chapter 1: Personal Influences

how they affected Eliot's representation of important themes.

Chapter 2: Major Themes

Chapter 3: Characters and Their Motivations

character, Nancy clearly endures a process of transformation that touches on pivotal themes in the novel.

FOREWORD

*"'Tis the good reader that
makes the good book."*

Ralph Waldo Emerson

The story's bare facts are simple: The captain, an old and scarred seafarer, walks with a peg leg made of whale ivory. He relentlessly drives his crew to hunt the world's oceans for the great white whale that crippled him. After a long search, the ship encounters the whale and a fierce battle ensues. Finally the captain drives his harpoon into the whale, but the harpoon line catches the captain about the neck and drags him to his death.

A simple story, a straightforward plot—yet, since the 1851 publication of Herman Melville's *Moby-Dick*, readers and critics have found many meanings in the struggle between Captain Ahab and the whale. To some, the novel is a cautionary tale that depicts how Ahab's obsession with revenge leads to his insanity and death. Others believe that the whale represents the unknowable secrets of the universe and that Ahab is a tragic hero who dares to challenge fate by attempting to discover this knowledge. Perhaps Melville intended Ahab as a criticism of Americans' tendency to become involved in well-intentioned but irrational causes. Or did Melville model Ahab after himself, letting his fictional character express his anger at what he perceived as a cruel and distant god?

Although literary critics disagree over the meaning of *Moby-Dick*, readers do not need to choose one particular interpretation in order to gain an understanding of Melville's novel. Instead, by examining various analyses, they can gain numerous insights into the issues that lie under the surface of the basic plot. Studying the writings of literary critics can also aid readers in making their own assessments of *Moby-Dick* and other literary works and in developing analytical thinking skills.

The Greenhaven Literary Companion Series was created with these goals in mind. Designed for young adults, this unique anthology series provides an engaging and comprehensive introduction to literary analysis and criticism. The essays included in the Literary Companion Series are chosen for their accessibility to a young adult audience and are expertly edited in consideration of both the reading and comprehension levels of this audience. In addition, each essay is introduced by a concise summation that presents the contributing writer's main themes and insights. Every anthology in the Literary Companion Series contains a varied selection of critical essays that cover a wide time span and express diverse views. Wherever possible, primary sources are represented through excerpts from authors' notebooks, letters, and journals and through contemporary criticism.

Each title in the Literary Companion Series pays careful consideration to the historical context of the particular author or literary work. In-depth biographies and detailed chronologies reveal important aspects of authors' lives and emphasize the historical events and social milieu that influenced their writings. To facilitate further research, every anthology includes primary and secondary source bibliographies of articles and/or books selected for their suitability for young adults. These engaging features make the Greenhaven Literary Companion Series ideal for introducing students to literary analysis in the classroom or as a library resource for young adults researching the world's great authors and literature.

Exceptional in its focus on young adults, the Greenhaven Literary Companion Series strives to present literary criticism in a compelling and accessible format. Every title in the series is intended to spark readers' interest in leading American and world authors, to help them broaden their understanding of literature, and to encourage them to formulate their own analyses of the literary works that they read. It is the editors' hope that young adult readers will find these anthologies to be true companions in their study of literature.

INTRODUCTION

Unfortunately, for many years George Eliot's *Silas Marner* has been assigned in high school English classes mainly because of its short length. Unlike Eliot's other lengthy novels, *Silas Marner* is barely two hundred pages (if that), a manageable length for a high school teacher trying to create a complete and well-rounded curriculum. Yet for many high school students *Silas Marner* seems two hundred pages too long. They question its relevance to their lives and find its ostensibly simple portrayal of Silas and the people of Raveloe unexciting and slow-moving. As Ken Sonenclar wrote in his article "Required Reading" in *New Leader:* "In 1971, I was suspended indefinitely from junior-year English for refusing to read George Eliot's classic. . . . I condemned *Marner* without reading a page. It wasn't necessary; the 19th century story of a weaver's life in a remote English village was obviously irrelevant." But as Sonenclar came to realize many years later: "I realized that *Silas Marner* is, after all, very much a tale of our times. Never slumping to melodrama, the story grapples with a multitude of contemporary problems—adultery, betrayal, substance abuse, deceit, mental illness, larceny, thievery, spiritual transformation. . . . It even takes a hard slap at Christian fundamentalism." Similarly, child psychiatrist Robert Coles believes that *Silas Marner*, properly taught, can relate to students of all economic backgrounds, especially if the teacher focuses on the novel's theme of the rebirth of a "lonely victimized individual."

George Eliot believed it is critical for one's development as a person to take responsibility for one's choices and to accept the consequences of one's actions. Eliot's moral code reflects the belief that seemingly minor choices of right or wrong can have severe moral and personal consequences. For students today, faced with so many "seemingly minor choices" of right or wrong it is important to remember that the results from those choices can profoundly affect or change one's life.

Thus, the many important social issues and themes which are the focus of Eliot's novel are still relevant today, and these are what makes *Silas Marner* worth reading. *Silas Marner* offers readers an opportunity to view for themselves what can become of one's own life when one makes the easy—and morally sloppy—choice, rather than the more difficult, but ultimately more rewarding, choice of moral integrity.

GEORGE ELIOT: A BIOGRAPHY

George Eliot was born Mary Anne Evans in 1819 in Warwickshire, England. It was in this country setting that she would later place many of her novels. Her father, Robert Evans, was the trusted land agent for the Newdigate family, a large landowner in Warwickshire. After Robert's first wife died, he married Christiana Pearson, who bore him three children: Christiana (Chrissey), Isaac, and Mary Anne. Robert also had two children from his first marriage. In 1820, when Mary Anne was a few months old, the entire family moved to Griff House on the Newdigate estate, where Eliot would live until she was twenty-one years old.

FAMILY TIES

Eliot was close to her father and cared for him until he died. From her letters, her pride in his vocation and her distress over his illnesses are evident. Less is known about her relationship with her mother, who died in 1836. As a child Eliot was extremely close to her brother, Isaac, a bond reflected in Maggie and Tom Tullivers' relationship in the novel *The Mill on the Floss*. (Similarly, her distress over later conflict with Isaac is reflected in Maggie and Tom Tullivers' own tragic quarrel.) Eliot's relationship with her sister, Chrissey, was also close.

CHILDHOOD AND EARLY ADULTHOOD

Eliot's childhood was spent at Griff House. She and her siblings were sent away to various boarding schools beginning in 1824. They returned home for the holidays, however, and spent their time in the usual childhood activities around the estate. Eliot's closest friend at this time was Maria Lewis, a governess at Nuneaton, one of the schools Eliot attended. At age sixteen, Eliot left school at Christmas 1835, when both her mother and father fell seriously ill. Her father recovered but her mother continued to decline and died in 1836. When

Chrissey married a year later, Eliot became the manager of her father's house. It was at this time that Eliot changed the spelling of her name to Mary Ann.[1]

Robert Evans retired in 1841. He moved with his daughter to Coventry, and Isaac took over as land agent for the Newdigate family. In Coventry, Eliot established new friendships and became interested in social reform. In 1844, encouraged by her new friends, she began a translation of theologian and philosopher David Friedrich Strauss's *Life of Jesus,* including the translation of passages in Greek and Hebrew as well as German into English. Eliot persevered with this work despite health problems, believing that Strauss offered an important statement on religion. Early in 1846, as she drew near the end of this difficult undertaking, her father fell ill again. He was to live another three years during which time Eliot was able to do much traveling and writing. She met American philosopher Ralph Waldo Emerson and magazine publisher John Chapman, traveled to London to attend concerts, and read a wide range of books from German and French philosophers to English novels to scientific treatises. Yet her responsibilities also lay with caring for her father. She had remained close to her father, and she wrote in a letter to her new friends, the Brays, "What shall I be without my father? It will seem as if a part of my moral nature were gone." Robert Evans died May 30, 1849, and was buried June 6, 1849, beside his wife. He divided his property between his two sons—Isaac and his half-brother, Robert— and left specific sums of money to his three daughters— Chrissey, Mary Anne, and their half-sister, Fanny. It was the income from this inheritance that Isaac oversaw and that Eliot would later share with Chrissey when she was in financial need.

After her father's death, Eliot traveled to the Continent with the Brays, but when her companions returned to England in July 1849, Eliot chose to remain in Switzerland until March 30, 1850. When she returned to England, she stayed for a time with her brother at Griff House, where he now lived, and with the Brays, while she considered what to do next.

---

1. Indeed, in her biography of George Eliot entitled *George Eliot: A Life,* Rosemary Ashton indicates that in the course of her life, George Eliot adopted three different spellings of her birth name, Mary Anne Evans. Each change, for Eliot, marked what she saw as a distinct change in her life and her fortunes.

RELIGIOUS DELIBERATIONS

As a child, Mary Anne was strongly influenced by the Puritan elements in the Anglican Church. Her friend Maria Lewis was involved in the movement and disapproved of excessive leisure and pleasure activities. Eliot's father was a traditional Anglican (member of the Church of England), but his brother Samuel had converted to Methodism in 1790. Indeed Samuel's wife, Elizabeth, was a Methodist preacher, and Eliot would later base the character of Dinah Morris, a woman preacher in *Adam Bede,* on this aunt, whom she respected. These influences led Eliot to be extremely judgmental in her youth. She refused to attend the theater with Isaac when they went to London in 1838 and harshly condemned religious writings and services that she felt were not appropriate. In *Silas Marner,* George Eliot would base Lantern Yard's characters and their actions on the values she absorbed through her Puritan interests.

But this strict religious morality did not last. By 1840, her wide reading led her to question some of her severe Puritan judgments. Then, with the move to Coventry, she was exposed to a wide diversity of religious thoughts. She struck up a friendship with the Bray and Hennell families, who were active in social and religious reform movements. Charles Hennell, the author of *Inquiry Concerning the Origin of Christianity,* a book questioning religious beliefs, was the brother of Cara Bray, her close friend. By January 1842, Eliot was questioning Christianity as prescribed by the Church of England, and on January 2, 1842, she refused to go to church with her father. Taking refuge at Isaac's house because of her father's anger, she wrote to her father: "While I admire and cherish much of what I believe to have been the moral teaching of Jesus himself, I consider the system of doctrines built upon the facts of his life . . . to be most dishonourable to God." She declared it would be hypocritical for her to attend church, and she would not do so. This decision would ultimately damage her friendship with Maria Lewis, who visited her in Coventry in 1842, and several months passed before she and her father were reconciled.

In the end, George Eliot developed a set of principles of her own, which she portrayed in her novels. These principles stressed individual responsibility for one's actions and freedom of will. People were good or evil based on their own actions, and the consequences of those actions could be irreversible. Indeed, Godfrey's choice early in *Silas Marner* not to recognize his responsibility to Eppie leads inevitably and relentlessly to Eppie's rejection of him as her father at the end of the novel.

ELIOT AND LEWES

Eliot moved to London to live in 1851. She boarded at the house of magazine publisher John Chapman, who had recently purchased the *Westminster Review*, a literary and political journal, and Eliot soon became an anonymous editor for the journal. At this time she also changed the spelling of her first name to Marian. Eliot continued to work for Chapman for several years, honing her skills as an editor and a writer. During this time she also met a large number of important intellectuals and writers, but the man who was to have the most influence on her was George Henry Lewes, whom she met in 1851.

Lewes was in his midthirties when they met. A novelist, playwright, and translator, he was fluent in French, German, and Spanish, and had a working knowledge of several other languages. He had written a survey of philosophy and at the time was working on a book about French philosopher Auguste Comte. Lewes was also married with three children. But Lewes's wife, Agnes, had a long-term relationship with Thornton Hunt, a political editor, by whom she had four children. Lewes knew of this relationship (as did much of London), and even registered two of Hunt's children as his own. Ultimately, according to English law, his acceptance of Hunt's children as his own rendered him ineligible to divorce Agnes on the grounds of adultery.

Thus by 1853, when Lewes and Eliot had fallen in love, their options were limited. They chose to live together as man and wife without being married, and Eliot took to signing her letters Marian Lewes. This decision stunned many of their friends and outraged others. For much of their time together, men would gather at their home to enjoy the intellectual discussions to be found there, but would not introduce or bring their wives. Even Eliot's friend Cara Bray, a reform thinker herself, had difficulty accepting Eliot and Lewes's relationship, and the two friends did not see each other for several years, although they did correspond through Bray's husband, Charles.

Eliot's brother, Isaac, strongly opposed the union, precipitating a lengthy estrangement. Yet despite their estrangement, Isaac conscientiously managed the money their father left Eliot at his death. Since the death of Chrissey's husband, Eliot helped support her and her children. But after her revelation to Isaac and Chrissey about her relationship with Lewes, Isaac prevailed on Chrissey to stop communicating with Eliot, even though Eliot continued to send Chrissey money. This breech lasted until Chrissey, dying of consumption in 1859, wrote to Eliot expressing regret that she had ever broken off the correspondence.

Lewes encouraged Eliot to begin writing novels, negotiated her publication contracts, and protected her from criticism. His importance in her emotional and intellectual growth and her development as an author cannot be overstressed. His brilliant mind and far-reaching interests gave her the intellectual stimulation she needed and the confidence to start writing fiction, as did his belief in Eliot's abilities and his willingness to shield her from criticism. Slowly, London society came to tolerate, if not accept, their relationship. Lewes's own sons became fond of Eliot and lived with the couple at various times. All the while, Lewes continued to support his wife, Agnes, and all of her children, which often left Lewes and Eliot financially strapped in the early years before their various successes as authors, hers in fiction and his in nonfiction. Indeed, Eliot claimed she took "George" as part of her pen name in honor of Lewes. Lewes and Eliot remained together until his death in 1878.

ELIOT'S FINAL YEARS

Eliot's last novel, *Daniel Deronda*, was finished in 1876, two years before Lewes's death. In poor health, Eliot and Lewes journeyed to the Continent as they often did after Eliot completed her novels. But when they both became sick, they changed their plans to go to Italy and instead spent much of their time in Switzerland and Germany before returning to England. They spent Lewes's final year traveling in England. In the summer of 1878, they occupied the country house they had recently purchased, and there Lewes's health declined precipitously. In November they returned to London where Lewes died on November 30. The funeral, which Eliot was too distraught to attend, was on December 4. With Lewes's death, Eliot assumed the revision of the final two volumes of Lewes's *Problems of Life and Mind*. She found herself rereading Queen Victoria's journal and empathizing with her grief on the death of Prince Albert. She also legally changed her last name to Lewes, so that she could establish and continue a studentship (financial grant) for scientists at Cambridge in his honor.

In early 1879 she began to visit friends again, particularly John Cross, her and Lewes's financial adviser. Cross's mother died shortly after Lewes, and the bereaved were able to comfort each other. Cross had long admired Eliot and they found themselves drawn together. On May 6, 1880, Eliot married John Cross, who was nearly twenty years younger than she. While some friends were shocked by this marriage, Lewes's sons and family were supportive of Eliot's decision, and Eliot was reconciled with her brother, Isaac, who considered her to have established a legitimate marriage. The marriage, however, was as controversial as Eliot's earlier choice to live with a married man. Whether or not it was a happy or contented marriage, it is difficult to say. Some accounts cite rumors that Cross showed signs of madness and that Eliot intended to leave him. But Eliot was already in poor health when Lewes died in 1878. On December 22, 1880, six months after marrying Cross, Eliot died of a throat infection and kidney problems. Despite the rumors of personal unhappiness, John Cross wrote of the loss of his "great wife" and five years later published his biography of Eliot.

ELIOT'S WRITINGS

George Eliot wrote eight major novels, a verse drama, several poems, essays, and short stories in her twenty-one-year career. All of her novels, except *Romola*, portray nineteenth-century England, and she set many of them in her childhood countryside of the Warwickshire Midlands. The novels, written during and after the late Industrial Revolution, contrast industrialization with agrarian values and lifestyles. They capture, as Rosemary Ashton states, "the discontinuities, contradictions, and bewilderment of the Victorian Age" and give "imaginative expression to the excitement and the pain of being caught up in a society in flux." Indeed, to the Victorians the postindustrial world was no longer a safe and ordered place. After 1848, when revolutions shook many of the thrones in Europe, there was a belief that worse might follow. Moreover, some had begun to perceive the destructive influence of industrialization. Benjamin Disraeli, prime minister under Queen Victoria, discussed "two nations," rich and poor, and voiced anxieties that these two groups were heading toward a violent meeting. These fears and confusions are reflected in Eliot's novels as she deals with issues as wide-ranging as gender discrimination, class intolerance, and religious intolerance.

Given the tensions within her own life, it is not surprising that Eliot emphasized in many of her novels the contrasting needs to question and rebel against established traditions and to belong and be accepted. Indeed, protagonists such as Maggie Tulliver in *The Mill on the Floss* illustrate the conflict within restrictive social codes and practices and the need to belong. In many of her novels, including *Adam Bede, The Mill on the Floss,* and *Middlemarch,* society is the framework or even active agent. Eliot describes a society confronted by change at every level and often delineates a series of characters who are constrained from what they believe is morally appropriate behavior. Eliot is also especially adept at portraying the emotional and moral difficulties of common, ordinary people. She emphasizes her characters' moral development, examining their internal motivations as well as their overt actions. This tendency toward in-depth analysis has led some critics to insist that her writing is, as Sidney Colvin claims, "impeded by excess of thought." But in reality, she brought a new intellectual standard to the novel, becoming what Virginia Woolf termed the "first English novelist to write exclusively for grown-ups." Eliot's novels illustrate the fate of individuals caught up in important events and major societal changes and show how the choices these individuals make determine the outcome of their own lives.

WRITING *SILAS MARNER*

In 1860, in the midst of researching material for *Romola,* Eliot found herself inspired by an idea that was to become her novel *Silas Marner.* The idea for *Silas Marner,* she stated, "thrust itself between me and the other book I was meditating." Eliot claimed in a letter to her publisher, John Blackwood, that the idea came to her "quite suddenly, as a sort of legendary tale, suggested by my recollection of having once, in early childhood, seen a linen weaver with a bag on his back." But she goes on to explain that having started with the idea of writing a legendary tale she "became inclined to a more realistic treatment." This dual inclination led her to write a novel that has the charm of a fairy tale and the strength of what Walter Allen terms "a completely created fictitious society." Certainly, the two elements of fairy tale and realism are inextricably entwined in the novel's confident delineation of the villagers and its portrayal of moral redemption.

Compared with Eliot's other works, the writing of *Silas Marner* went smoothly and rather quickly. Certainly, it was a more enjoyable experience than her next novel, *Romola*, which she found to be difficult and stressful. Biographer Rosemary Ashton states that, as much as George Eliot could relax with any novel, she did so with *Silas Marner*, and it was produced with less despair than any other of her works.

The novel itself is set during the Napoleonic Wars, although the conflict only peripherally affects the story's action. The more important historical events are those of the industrialization of England's labor force and the growth in dissenting (non–Church of England) Protestant sects. These historical events can be seen in Silas's early life in Lantern Yard, his occupation as a linen weaver, and the later displacement of Lantern Yard by a factory. The plot of the novel traces the fortunes of two men: Silas Marner and Godfrey Cass. Eliot's belief that one's moral choices in life determine life's outcome can be seen in the actions of both men. Over the course of sixteen years, their fortunes and happiness are inverted by the moral decisions each one of them makes.

ELIOT'S PERSONALITY

George Eliot was by the standards of her day physically unattractive; her appearance worried her in her early years. Some have suggested that the early attraction between Eliot and Lewes was based on their physical plainness, but it is more likely that intellectual superiority attracted each to the other. Eliot's intellect cannot be denied. As Oscar Browning wrote about visiting her in his book *Life of George Eliot:*

> Her conversation was deeply sympathetic, but grave and solemn, illumined by happy phrases and thrilling tenderness, but not by humour. Although her features were heavy, and not well proportioned, all was forgotten when that majestic head bent slowly down, and the eyes were lit up with a penetrating and lively gaze. She appeared much greater than her books. Her ability seemed to shrink beside her moral grandeur. She was not only the cleverest, but the best woman you had met.

Rosemary Ashton, in her biography of George Eliot, concludes that Eliot is a difficult woman to categorize. She was insecure and extremely sensitive to criticism. Writing, while the marrow of her life, did not always come easily to her, and she agonized over the best and most effective manner in which to convey her ideas in many of the later novels. Yet, despite her sensitivity to criticism, she was a strong-minded and highly principled woman who defied her family and society at large to live the life she believed to be right for her. As Ashton emphasizes, while Eliot was not the first woman to pursue a writing career, "The distinctiveness of [her] life—the particular turns it took, the successive milieus she inhabited, the shock waves caused in respectable, orthodox social circles by some of her actions—needs to be stressed. Nowadays few bat an eyelid at young people, and young women in particular, professing no religious faith, pursuing studies and careers. Marian Evans did these things, yet as others observed of her, and as she herself recognized, her temperament was at bottom one which sought approval and desired to conform."

Her contemporaries, torn between awe at her knowledge and disapproval over her lifestyle, were equally unsure how to judge her. Herbert Spencer, a friend of both Eliot and Lewes, wrote of Eliot that she was "the most admirable woman, mentally, I ever met." William Hale White, an author and editor for Chapman, said of her: "She was really one of the most sceptical, unusual creatures I ever knew, and it was this side of her character which to me was the most attractive." She was greatly admired by academics, writers, and philosophers for her intellect, her depth and breadth of knowledge, and her strength of character. Yet the criticism of her personal life was often apparent. Eliza Lynn Linton, a former writer for the *Westminster Review* for whom Eliot had little regard, related this telling incident, when, "Lewes and George Eliot once thought of establishing a domicile [home] in Kent . . . a council of male and female heads of families was held to decide whether George Eliot should be 'received.' It was decided that she should not."

In the end, perhaps it was the conflict of needs and strength of character in Eliot's own personality that gave her the compassion and perception to create the sensitive and isolated characters found in her novels, such as Silas himself in *Silas Marner.*

CHARACTERS AND PLOT

MAJOR CHARACTERS

Godfrey Cass: The squire's elder son and a member of the gentry class, Godfrey loves Nancy Lammeter but has secretly married Molly, a barmaid, and fathered a baby girl, the same child who has through circumstance been adopted by Silas. Godfrey wishes to be freed from his foolish marriage but is afraid to admit to his mistake. When Molly dies on her way to Squire Cass's house to confront Godfrey, Godfrey is relieved that he need not admit to their marriage and is now free to marry Nancy Lammeter. Consequently, he chooses not to claim the baby girl Silas has adopted as his own daughter. Many years later, after Godfrey has married Nancy and they have failed to have any children of their own, he tells Nancy about Eppie's lineage. They go to Silas's cottage and reveal Godfrey's secret, planning to take Eppie home with them, but it is too late. Eppie rejects Godfrey and chooses to remain with Silas.

Eppie: The child Silas adopts after his gold is stolen, Eppie is the biological daughter of Godfrey Cass and the barmaid Molly. However, Eppie grows up not knowing that Godfrey Cass is her father as he is afraid to admit to his disastrous marriage to Molly. Eppie enjoys the complete love and devotion of Silas and returns his affections completely. When Godfrey tries to claim her as his daughter, Eppie states clearly that Silas is her true father, regardless of her true parentage. Finally when she and Aaron Winthrop fall in love and plan to marry, she is quite clear that they must live with Silas and care for him in his old age.

Silas Marner: A linen weaver by trade, Silas has exiled himself from Lantern Yard, the religious community where he had lived, after being falsely condemned of stealing a dying deacon's money. An epileptic who has been told his fits are curses from God, Silas takes refuge in the small village of Raveloe. At first, he is a reclusive miser shunned by the villagers for his disability and his odd, solitary ways. But when Silas's gold is stolen, he is accepted by the villagers, and when a small orphaned child finds her way to his hearth, he chooses to adopt her. Through Silas's love for this child, Eppie, he becomes a part of the community as he is transformed from a reclusive miser into a loving, giving man.

MINOR CHARACTERS

Dunsey Cass: The squire's dissolute younger son; he is blackmailing Godfrey over his foolish marriage.

Squire Cass: The "greatest man" in the village of Raveloe; a widowed landowner, he lives in a large red brick house and has two sons.

William Dane: A friend of Silas's at Lantern Yard; he steals the dying deacon's money and frames Silas for the crime.

Mr. Dowlas: A patron of the Rainbow, Raveloe's local pub.

Doctor and Mrs. Kimble: Members of the gentry who visit with the Cass family.

Nancy Lammeter: The daughter of a neighboring landowner; she loves Godfrey and marries him, unaware of his past.

Priscilla Lammeter: Nancy's sister; she has decided to remain unmarried and care for her family.

Mr. Macey: Tailor and parish clerk; he befriends Silas in his distress over his stolen money and also plays the fiddle at Squire Cass's Christmas ball.

Molly: The barmaid who Godfrey marries; she is addicted to opium. She travels to Raveloe to confront Godfrey with his neglect and their child, but she collapses and dies near Silas's cottage before she can see Godfrey.

Mr. and Mrs. Osgood: Members of the gentry who visit with the Cass family.

The peddler: A traveling seller of goods, such as ribbons, pots, and pans; he is originally assumed to have stolen Silas's money.

Jem Rodney: A patron of the Rainbow, Raveloe's local pub.

Sarah: Silas's fiancee at Lantern Yard; Silas assumes she will reject him after his condemnation for theft. Later she marries William Dane.

Aaron Winthrop: Dolly's son, who loves Eppie.

Ben Winthrop: A patron of the Rainbow, Raveloe's local pub.

Dolly Winthrop: Silas's neighbor in Raveloe, the good-hearted wife of the wheelwright who attempts to befriend Silas. After Silas adopts Eppie, Dolly functions as both adviser and friend.

PLOT SUMMARY

Silas Marner is set in England during the years 1795 to 1816. At the story's outset Silas Marner, a linen weaver, has lived in the countryside village of Raveloe for fifteen years. Despite this length of time, he remains detached from village society. He is never found in The Rainbow, the local pub, or seen gossiping with his neighbors. Silas's inability to fit into life at Raveloe stems from his earlier experiences at Lantern Yard, the religious community where he used to live and work. At Lantern Yard, his closest friend was William Dane and his fiancée was Sarah, a young serving girl. But William was not a true friend, and he soon turned on Silas. The weaver suffers from epilepsy, and William decided to use the community's ignorance of this disorder to cast Silas in a poor light. William suggested to the church's congregation that Silas's epileptic fits were visitations from Satan, and the community became instantly suspicious of the weaver. During one particular fit, Silas was attending a dying deacon. William Dane chose the moment to steal the deacon's savings and frame the defenseless Silas. With the community already convinced of his link to the devil, Silas could turn to no one to plead his innocence. The local congregation held a makeshift trial and found Silas guilty. Sarah immediately broke off her engagement and soon afterward married William Dane. An outcast from his community, Silas left Lantern Yard soon after the wedding, and after wandering through the countryside, settled in Raveloe. Lantern Yard's assumption of his guilt and consequent rejection of the weaver left Silas suspicious of human contact. And in Raveloe, Silas keeps isolated from other members of the community. Consequently the villagers of Raveloe shun Silas and are somewhat afraid of him. They also do not understand Silas's epileptic fits and see them as an evil portent. Jem Rodney, the mole-catcher, once saw Silas standing with his eyes like a "dead man's" and his limbs rigid and reported this to others in Raveloe, feeding the local superstitions. In addition, one of the few times Silas interacted with his neighbors was when he helped cure Sally Oates. Although his familiarity with herbal remedies saved the girl, the demonstration of such arcane knowledge made the villagers doubly suspicious of him.

While Silas does not become a part of the village of Raveloe, his skill as a weaver allows him to work steadily. His isolation, however, fosters rumors that the successful weaver must have a great fortune hidden in his home. Indeed, alone in Raveloe, Silas has been slowly building up a large fortune of gold pieces. And because he has no friends, Silas forms an attachment to his money. His coins become his only companions, and he keeps them well hidden in an iron pot in the floor under his loom.

Paralleling the early narrative about Silas Marner is the story of Godfrey Cass, the son of a local squire whose family owns land in the Raveloe countryside. Squire Cass, whose wife has long since died, has two sons, Godfrey and Dunstan (Dunsey). Godfrey, the eldest, is well liked by the villagers and the other landowners. Dunsey, however, is a nasty young man who drinks and gambles too much. Most of the neighbors expect that Godfrey will marry Nancy Lammeter, the daughter of a neighbor whom he obviously loves. But what no one knows except Dunsey is that Godfrey had already secretly married a barmaid named Molly and fathered a baby daughter. Molly, however, was a less-than suitable mate with an alcohol and drug problem. Godfrey has regretted for a long while his secret marriage to the barmaid, but is afraid to confess his foolishness to his father who might disinherit him. Moreover, Dunsey is blackmailing Godfrey, knowing of Godfrey's love for Nancy and his fear of his father's reaction. In fact, Godfrey gave Dunsey money from one of his father's tenant's rent payments, and now his father is asking where the rent money is. Dunsey tells Godfrey that Godfrey must sell his hunting horse to recover the money, as Dunsey has none of it left, and he offers to take the horse to a local hunt, show it off during the hunt, and then sell it there. But while riding the horse at the hunt, irresponsible Dunsey miscalculates jumping over a fence and the horse is killed.

Walking home from the hunt, Dunsey passes Silas Marner's cottage and recalls rumors of the fortune Marner has hoarded. Silas has momentarily stepped away from the cottage, leaving the door open, and his hiding space uncovered.

Dunsey walks in, sees the hole in the floor, and steals Silas's gold. Silas returns to his cottage and discovers the missing money. In shock, he searches the cottage, then staggers off into the village and ends up at the pub, the Rainbow. The local villagers are passing time at the pub when Silas enters, staring like a ghost and moaning about his money. When the villagers realize what Silas is talking about, they urge him to go to the constable's house to report the stolen gold.

The next day villagers and landowners alike discuss the theft of Silas's gold and speculate about who might have stolen the money. No suspicion falls on Dunsey, even though he has not returned home. Indeed, when it is discovered that he has killed Godfrey's horse at the hunt, Godfrey assumes he has gone off in anger. Godfrey confesses to his father he gave Dunsey the rent money and his father, though angry, does nothing more than yell at him. Meanwhile, the villagers have taken pity on Silas because of his loss. In particular, Dolly Winthrop, a neighbor and the wheelwright's wife, visits him with her young son Aaron to wish him a merry Christmas, as the holidays have come upon the village.

In the spirit of Christmas, Squire Cass hosts a Christmas ball at which he and many others expect Godfrey to propose to Nancy Lammeter. Though relieved that Dunsey has disappeared, Godfrey knows he cannot marry Nancy while he is legally married to Molly. He still is afraid to confess to his father that he has made this secret and foolish marriage.

While Godfrey is dancing with Nancy at the ball, his wife Molly makes her way to the squire's house with their baby daughter to confront Godfrey. Numbed by the cold and snow, addled by laudanum she collapses near Silas Marner's cottage. The baby girl crawls away from her mother and into the warmth of the cottage. Silas catches sight of the child's golden hair; at first, being nearsighted, he thinks his gold has come back to him. Then he recognizes a child is at his hearth, and he steps outside to find the mother lying in the snow.

Silas goes to the squire's house to fetch the doctor, interrupting the Christmas ball. When he announces his find, many return with him to his cottage, including Godfrey. The doctor declares the woman is dead. Godfrey recognizes his wife and his daughter but he lacks the moral courage to claim them as his own. Instead, he is relieved, believing he is free to marry Nancy. Silas, to the surprise of many, takes the child in to raise himself, naming her Eppie after a younger sister who has died.

As Part I of the novel ends, Silas has entered the life of the village, through Eppie, and Godfrey marries Nancy, without revealing that Eppie is his child.

Part II opens sixteen years after the end of Part I. Silas's fortunes have continued to grow. His love for Eppie and her love for him have softened him and redeemed him in the community. Aaron, Dolly Winthrop's son, who is in love with Eppie, is helping her build a garden with rocks from an old quarry nearby. Silas has begun attending the local church for Eppie's sake, and the villagers' opinions of Silas have changed completely.

Meanwhile, Godfrey's good fortune is dimmed; though happy in their marriage, Godfrey and Nancy have had no children. Godfrey once broached to Nancy the possibility of adopting Eppie, but Nancy turned the suggestion down, unaware of Eppie's true identity. Godfrey takes comfort in the fact that Dunsey has never returned; of course, no one knows that Dunsey stole Silas's money.

Then the quarry from which Aaron is fetching rocks for Eppie's garden goes dry and a body is exposed. It is Dunsey's body, and discovered next to the body is Silas's stolen gold. Apparently after the theft, Dunsey fell into the quarry in the dark and was killed. Godfrey is horrified to learn that it was his brother who stole Silas's money, and remorsefully confesses to Nancy the truth about Molly and Eppie. Nancy is upset, not because of the confession but because Godfrey did not trust her with the truth.

The couple decides to go to Silas Marner's cottage the next day and reveal Eppie's identity, hoping to return with her to their home and the comforts they can provide. At first, they offer to raise Eppie without naming Godfrey as her father, but Eppie refuses their offer. Then, when Godfrey confesses the truth, Silas berates him for his moral cowardice sixteen years ago, a chastisement Godfrey accepts. Nevertheless he insists on his rights as Eppie's natural father, so Silas allows Eppie to choose her future.

Eppie very kindly thanks them for their generous offer but makes it clear her heart and place are with Silas. Godfrey leaves abruptly and Nancy follows. As they walk away, Godfrey sadly acknowledges to Nancy that he gave away the true riches he could have had sixteen years ago and he will never regain them.

After this confrontation, Silas decides to revisit the community of his childhood and young adulthood, Lantern Yard. He sets out with Eppie but discovers the community has disappeared without a trace. In its place is a large new factory. Silas returns to Raveloe content with his life. Eppie and Aaron marry and live with Silas.

CHAPTER 1

Personal Influences

READINGS ON
SILAS MARNER

The Psychological Contexts of Eliot's Writing of *Silas Marner*

Peggy Fitzhugh Johnstone

In this article, Peggy Fitzhugh Johnstone examines psychological aspects of *Silas Marner.* Although she does discuss Silas's compulsive behavior and his subsequent cure, Johnstone concentrates on Eliot's psychological motivations in writing *Silas Marner,* including her relationships with her brothers, sisters, and parents. Johnstone ends the article by comparing Eliot's family relationships with those of Silas Marner and hypothesizes how *Silas Marner* may reflect Eliot's own family ties. This article was later reprinted in Peggy Fitzhugh Johnstone's book, *The Transformation of Rage: Mourning and Creativity in George Eliot's Fiction.* The book is a part of the Literature and Psychoanalysis series edited by Jeffrey Berman.

In September 1860—a few months after she had completed *The Mill on the Floss,* and was preparing to write *Romola*— George Eliot had an idea which "thrust itself'" upon her. The result was her short novel, *Silas Marner,* which she completed by 4 March 1861 and which she described to her editor as a story that "came to me, quite suddenly, as a sort of legendary tale, suggested by my recollection of having once, in my early childhood, seen a linen weaver with a bag on his back." In keeping with Eliot's account of the curious nature or the work's genesis, and in view both of the novel's relative brevity and the rapidity with which it was composed, critics have tended to regard *Silas Marner* as "uncharacteristic" and have typically treated it as an interruption on the path toward the writing of her major works.

From a psychoanalytic perspective, however, the very fact

Excerpted from "Loss, Anxiety, and Cure: Mourning and Creativity in *Silas Marner,*" by Peggy Fitzhugh Johnstone, *Mosaic,* 1992. Reprinted with permission.

that this novel seems to be a departure from Eliot's usual practice constitutes a compelling reason for giving it special attention. My purpose in the following essay, therefore, is to examine the personal factors that surrounded Eliot's composition of the work and to account for the novel's genesis by relating its concern with the theme of betrayal to the pain of losses that Eliot had repressed. . . .

SILAS'S COMPULSIVE BEHAVIOR

In *Silas Marner*, the isolated lifestyle of the protagonist is presented as a long-term reaction to a series of painful losses that had occurred fifteen years earlier. As a result of his betrayal by his best friend, William Dane, Silas had been unjustly accused of theft, cast out of his religious sect, and rejected by his fiancée, Sarah, who then married William. Having left the urban community of Lantern Yard, Silas came to live alone as a weaver in the rural village of Raveloe.

In Raveloe, without a sense of connection to family, friends or community, Silas's work has lost its purpose. His weaving becomes "an end in itself . . . [a] bridge over the loveless chasms of his life," and takes the form of the "unquestioning activity of a spinning insect." His money, formerly "the symbol of earthly good," also becomes important for its own sake. Feeling the gold coins "in his palm" and looking at "their bright faces" every evening becomes his greatest pleasure.

After he is robbed of the gold coins that had come to mean so much to him, Silas develops the habit of opening the door and "looking out from time to time," as though he hoped to see or hear of his money: "It was chiefly at night, when he was not occupied in his loom, that he fell into this repetition of an act for which he could have assigned no definite purpose, and which can hardly be understood except by those who have undergone a bewildering separation from a supremely loved object." Silas would look out "not with hope, but with mere yearning and unrest."

Eliot's presentation of repetition as Silas's reaction to the loss of a "supremely loved object" thus incisively anticipates Freud's elaboration of the concept of the repetition-compulsion. In *Beyond the Pleasure Principle*, Freud describes the repetitive game of "disappearance and return" invented by a toddler, age one and a half, in response to separations from his mother. Freud then explains the connection between the toddler's repetitive game and an adult's compulsion to repeat, which is a response to "narcissistic injury," or to painful experience which the mind interprets as loss of love. The aim of the repetition is to make the passive experience active, or, in other words, to "master" it. . . .

William's accusatory behavior, quickly followed by his feeling of "anxiety" over the possible loss of Sarah's love, suggests the close connection between anxiety over impending loss and the defensive process of repressing anger. Silas's fear of losing attachments renders him unable to assert himself against William, who had played the dominating role in their friendship. In the account of the events leading up to his departure from Lantern Yard, Silas's "impressible self-doubting nature" and "trusting simplicity" are contrasted with William's "over-severity towards weaker brethren" and self-assurance. Unwilling to admit any hostility toward his close friend, Silas complies too easily with William's theft of his fiancée. Throughout the novel, Silas is portrayed as a gentle person, incapable of hurting others. After Eppie, the orphaned toddler, enters his life, "he trembled at a moment's contention with her, lest she should love him the less for it." His decision to rear her "without punishment" is part of his pattern of disallowing any negative feelings toward loved ones for fear of losing them. In an ongoing circle, the fear of loss of love, or separation anxiety, itself provokes the aggressive impulses that must then be denied.

Fear of aggressive impulses is a prominent feature of what psychologists now call the obsessive-compulsive disorder—an anxiety disorder characterized by the sustained experience of repetitive actions and/or thoughts. According to a phenomenological analysis of the disorder by Salmon Akhtar, the most common forms of compulsions are washing, cleaning, counting and checking. Among the many forms of obsessions are repetitive thoughts, doubts, impulses or images, typically about subjects like dirt and/or contamination, aggression, sex, or religion.

In *Silas Marner,* Eliot vividly portrays her protagonist's compulsive behavior. She writes that Silas's "first movement after the shock [of being cast out of the congregation] had been to work at his loom; and he went on with this unremittingly." She then goes on to delineate the connection between Silas's compulsive weaving and the development of his obsession for gold. She compares him to men "shut up in solitary imprisonment" who keep track of intervals of time with marks on the wall, "until the growth of the sum of straight strokes, arranged in triangles, has become a mastering purpose." "That will help us to understand," she goes on, "how the love of accumulating money grows [into] all absorbing passion in men whose imaginations, even in the very beginning of their hoard, showed them no purpose beyond it." His "money had come to mark off his weaving into periods, and the money not only grew, but it remained with him." His compulsive actions ("unremitting" weaving during the day and ritualistic counting every night) and his obsession for gold seem to form a tightly bound circuit in which each continually reinforces the other. . . .

In Eliot's portrayal, it is Silas's sense of abandonment that drives him to turn the gold into a replacement for prior attachments. The coins become his companions: "He handled them, he counted them, till their form and colour were like the satisfaction of a thirst to him"; he "*clung* with all the force of his nature to his work and his money." The more Silas devotes himself to work and money, the more he takes on their qualities. Becoming like an inanimate object himself, he develops a "monotonous craving" for the "monotonous response" of the loom; "His gold, as he hung over it and saw it grow, gathered his power of loving together into a hard isolation like its own." The gold becomes a symbol of both the longing and the aggression (Freud's love-hate) felt toward a lost love.

SILAS'S "CURE"

Eliot's portrayal of Silas's cure, in turn, is in keeping with the psychoanalytic model advanced by Otto Fenichel, who explains that "upsetting" and "unforeseen" events can break through the obsessive-compulsive system, and serve as the source of "traumatic cure" of a "compulsive character." In *Silas Marner*, the theft of Silas's bag of gold coins is the unforeseen event that precipitates his cure. At first he cannot believe that the gold is really gone; he can feel "only terror, and the eager effort to put an end to the terror." Then, after a search of his cottage convinces him of the reality, he "put his trembling hands to his head, and gave a wild ringing scream, the cry of desolation. For a few moments after, he stood motionless; but the cry had relieved him from the first maddening pressure of the truth." Later, in a reflective passage elaborating the change in Silas, Eliot writes that Silas's "disposition to hoard" was "utterly crushed" by his "sense of bereavement." He had lost the symbol which had satisfied his "need for clinging. . . . Now the support was snatched away," and he was forced to feel all the pain of loss that had earlier been repressed: "He filled up the blank with grief."

The theft of the gold serves as a cure because, as a symbol for prior attachments, it provides Silas with a means of re-experiencing and ultimately resolving earlier losses. The loss of his fiancée had created the need to repeat its pattern in order to resolve it: by leaving his front door unlocked, Silas allows the thief to steal his coins, much as he had earlier allowed William to steal his fiancée. This time, however, he finds a more constructive way to respond to his pain. Instead of isolating himself, he goes out into the community and asks for help. Through talking with others, particularly with Dolly Winthrop, the neighbor who serves the function of a supportive therapist, he slowly reestablishes his sense of connection with others and with his own past. The sense or emptiness felt after the theft of the gold is finally filled by emotional ties, in particular by his relationship with his adopted daughter Eppie. When Marner first discovers Eppie, he thinks, "The child was come instead of the gold . . . the gold had turned into the child." Eliot goes on to elaborate: "The gold had kept his thoughts in an ever-repeat[ing] circle, leading to nothing beyond itself; but Eppie was an object compacted of changes and hopes that forced his thoughts onward."

Through his connection to the child, Silas also rediscovers his own childhood. His involvement with the strict religious sect at Lantern Yard had caused him to lose sight of his legacy from his mother: "some acquaintance with medicinal herbs and their preparation—a little store of wisdom which she had imparted to him as a solemn bequest." He had come to have "doubts about the lawfulness of applying this knowledge . . . so that his inherited delight to wander through the fields in search of foxglove and dandelion and coltsfoot, began to wear to him the character of a temptation." Through Eppie, Silas recovers what Brian Swann calls his "true past," and his "childlike vision" is restored. Silas, whose sense of self had depended to a great extent on his environment, finally grows into what Cohen terms "a new sense of wholeness" or what Shuttleworth terms "into the community and into a sense of continuity with the past."

ELIOT'S RELATIONSHIP WITH HER SIBLINGS

Biographical evidence, along with evidence derived from the patterns in her early fiction, suggests that through writing *Silas Marner,* Eliot was working through losses of her own. According to Gordon Haight, Eliot experienced "intense sadness" during the period before and during the writing of *Silas Marner,* and he attributes her "malaise and languor" to her "equivocal marital state"—that is, to her liaison with George Henry Lewes, who was married, although permanently separated from his wife, and unable to obtain a divorce. Since 1857, when she had written her family of her decision to live with Lewes, she had been a "complete outcast" from them. Her older brother Isaac, refusing to respond to her letter himself, communicated his displeasure through a family lawyer; at the same time, he pressured their half-sister Fanny and their sister Chrissey to send letters breaking off all communication.

The strength of Eliot's childhood attachment to her brother Isaac is well-known. . . . Yet judging from her letters, as an adult Eliot felt closer to her sister Chrissey. In letters to friends she mentions her sister's marriage, and the births and illnesses of her children, whereas references to her brother Isaac are relatively rare. Ruby Redinger reports that upon her return from a trip to the continent following her father's death, Eliot wrote her friend Cara Bray that "Dear Chrissey is much kinder than any one else in the family and I am happiest with her. She is generous and sympathizing and really cares for my happiness." Later, when Chrissey's husband died, leaving her with a large family, Eliot became increasingly concerned about her sister's welfare, and more than once expressed her desire to help her financially. In a letter to Isaac, she asked him to pay Chrissey fifteen pounds of her own income so that her sister might take a trip. In a letter to her friend Sara Hennell at about the same time, she wrote that she cared the most about staying in touch with Chrissey so that she would be able to help her, although at the time her financial capacity to do so was very limited.

In 1859, . . . she finally received a letter from Chrissey, who was very ill, and who expressed regret that she had "ever ceased to write . . . one who under all circumstances was kind to me and mine." When Chrissey died shortly after, Eliot, who had already written Sara Hennell that "The past is abolished from my mind—I only want [Chrissey] to feel that I love her and care for her," subsequently wrote that she "had a very special feeling" toward her sister.

Chrissey died in March 1859, when Eliot was beginning work on *The Mill on the Floss,* and just as she was approaching the tenth anniversary of her father's death, which had occurred in May 1849. In the light of Bowlby's explanation of the way that a recent loss, or the anniversary of a loss, or both, can activate repressed feelings of grief for an earlier one, I would argue that Eliot's sense of estrangement from her family intensified her grief (and, especially in light of her own current success, perhaps guilt) over her sister's misfortunes and death—a death which, because of its timing, revived feelings, however long repressed, associated with her parent's death.

The sibling attachment that is elaborated in *The Mill on the Floss* is only alluded to in *Silas Marner,* but is still at the core of the central character's psychological situation. Moreover, the sibling attachment in both novels is tied to earlier loss. . . . In *Silas Marner,* Silas finds in the golden-haired toddler, Eppie, a replacement for "his little sister whom he had carried about in his arms for a year before she died, when he was a small boy." He tells Dolly in a later conversation that his little sister had been named after his mother, Hephzibah. Thus his new love for his adopted child Eppie is linked not only to his lost sister, but to his mother, although it is the sibling attachment that is most clearly remembered.

ELIOT'S RELATIONSHIP WITH HER MOTHER

Eliot's childhood attachment to her older brother has led critics and biographers to ask questions about her relationship with her mother. In his early *Life of Eliot,* John Walter Cross had emphasized Eliot's grief over her mother's death, but noting that "letters for the two years following the mother's death are missing," Redinger concludes that "there is no objective evidence about George Eliot's memory of her mother." Haight intimates that Eliot experienced a poor relationship with her mother, but he provides no support for his contentions that "her mother's favorites were Isaac and Chrissey" and that "her mother had never been very close to Mary Anne." I would like to argue that Eliot's noted "paucity of comment about her mother" (Haight 22) is the silence of repression of painful affect in response to the loss of her mother—a loss which she associated with the death of siblings.

When Eliot was about sixteen months old, her mother gave birth to twins, who died when they were ten days old. After that, her mother "had not been well"—a circumstance which probably explains the development of her intense attachment to her older brother Isaac, "the dominating passion of her childhood," as Haight describes it. Eliot's mother, who appears to have been virtually missing in her daughter's life after that time, died when she was sixteen. The timing of the deaths was such that they occurred during critical stages in Eliot's development: the death of the twins occurred during a time when a child is still dependent on her mother's reliable presence for her own developing sense of her self; the death of her mother, during Mary Anne's adolescence, occurred at a time when early childhood stages are revived as part of the process of working toward adult identity. . . .

If Eliot's early childhood after the death of the twins was indeed "dominated" by her passion for her brother, then the fact that she was sent to a boarding school at age five involved a double loss—of both mother and brother. Haight writes of this time in 1824 that "Mary Anne never forgot her suffering . . . and her fears at night." Although there seems to be little information regarding the period of her life that immediately followed, Haight mentions that her brother, who was attending a different school, began to grow away from her, and that Mary Anne was forced to turn to books for solace. He then describes the way others saw her by 1827: "A very serious child" whose "unusual gravity" prompted the older girls to call her "little Mamma"; a child who did not like to be "made untidy," who suffered from "night terrors," who was "sensitive" and "easily reduced to passionate tears," and who came to be known for her preference for adults over children. . . .

In *Beyond the Pleasure Principle*, Freud gives examples of how the compulsion to repeat operates in the lives of adults—such as "the man whose friendships all end in betrayal by his friend" or "the lover each of whose love affairs . . . passes through the same phases and reaches the same conclusion." The adult compulsion to repeat also seems to characterize the pattern of Eliot's response to losses in her family. Haight records that when Eliot's mother died in 1836, her adolescent religious zeal "increased" and was accompanied by a determined self-denial. Her response to her father's death thirteen years later repeated the pattern, although in the latter case it involved an intense interest in Thomas à Kempis, whom she admired for his emphasis on "renunciation." Eliot seems to have reenacted the loss of her parents by temporarily identifying with an ideal that would then necessitate further loss.

A similar compulsion to repeat links Eliot's fiction to her reaction to Chrissey's death. Eliot's creation of the golden-haired toddler Eppie reflects her mind's attempt to rework the period of her childhood when she first experienced the loss of her mother that followed the death of her twin siblings. The idealized Eppie, who represents both sibling and mother to Silas, can also be seen as a symbol of Eliot's idealized self, reunited with mother, father and siblings, all represented by Silas. Just as Eppie brings back to Silas "a dreamy feeling, [with] . . . old quiverings of tenderness—old impressions of awe at the presentiment of some Power presiding over his life," so she provides for Eliot a means of recreating the symbiosis with the lost mother that Mahler believes it is part of the human condition to crave.

Yet at the same time, in *Silas Marner* the need to leave the mother and the past is also dramatized. When Eppie's mother, a drug addict with no remaining capacity to care for her child, dies, the child shows no sign of fear. With "the ready transition of infancy" (like Mahler's infants in the second subphase, practicing to move away from the mother by crawling and walking), Eppie turns easily from her dead mother's body; starting out on "all fours," she rises to her feet and toddles toward the light gleaming from the door of Silas's cottage. She is soon discovered by Silas, who cares for her, is allowed by the villagers to keep her, and then raises her "without punishment." Eppie and Silas continue to maintain their close attachment even after she grows up and marries a young man from the village. Thus, at the same time that *Silas Marner* expresses Eliot's wish to be reunited with her family, it also expresses her wish to separate painlessly from her deceased mother (in thie sense of leaving behind her grief over her loss), and to find a new, lasting love. . . .

SILAS MARNER AS A REFLECTION OF ELIOT'S RELATIONSHIPS

Certainly Eliot's life with Lewes allowed her to find her identify as a fiction writer—a vocation which depended on "the inspiriting influence of his constant encouragement" (Haight quoting Edith Simcox). Furthermore, her life of alienation from family and society simply allowed her the time she needed to write. Perhaps what Eliot was expressing in *Silas Marner* was her own "ready transition" from familial attachments to her new relationship with Lewes.

Toward the end of *Silas Marner*, Silas returns to Lantern Yard to try to talk to the minister of his old congregation. He wants to ask some questions about the past, in particular about the "drawing of the lots" (the method the congregation had used to determine his guilt), and to tell the minister "about the religion o' this countryside, for I partly think he doesn't know on it." When he arrives in town and looks around, he discovers that "Lantern Yard's gone." As he tells Dolly Winthrop upon his return to Raveloe, "The old home's gone; I've no home but this now. I shall never know whether they got at the truth o' the robbery, nor whether Mr. Paston could ha' given me any light about the drawing o' the lots. It's dark to me, Mrs. Winthrop, that is; I doubt it'll be dark to the last." Silas feels that he has been wronged in some way that he will never understand. His sense of loss, more than simple grief, is a mix of feelings, even including moral outrage. Yet he concludes that, from now on, Eppie's presence will give him "light enough to trusten by."

Silas and Eppie, as unlike each other as they appear to be, are characters who mirror one another. The change in Silas's psychological state is dramatized not only in his story, but in hers. Eppie, the idealized character, does easily what Silas, the realistically portrayed character, accomplishes only with great pain; she acts out literally what Silas must do indirectly, through a process of symbolization. Eppie readily turns away from her dead mother, while Silas is forced, only when his gold coins are stolen, to turn away from the "dead disrupted thing" which had satisfied his need for "clinging." The scene in which Eppie walks away from her mother is juxtaposed with the scene in which Silas repeatedly goes to the door to look for his lost gold, his "supremely loved object"; thus the two characters are brought together on the basis of their shared loss. Moreover, just as Eppie acts out what Silas needs to do, so Silas feels the pain that Eppie denies. Through the interaction of the mirroring characters, the novel makes the connection between the act of separation and the pain of loss. *Silas Marner* is among other things, then, a story about the pain of separating from maternal attachment.

If it is true, as I have argued, that Eliot was engaged in her own struggle to work through a too early and abrupt loss of maternal closeness, then her own mind, in "thrusting" upon her a story which would enact the process she needed to re-live, provided her with an indirect, symbolic means of get-ting at painful material from her past. According to Freud, the repetition-compulsion that is observable in children's play can also be observed in artistic creation. "Artistic play" is a means of "making what is in itself unpleasurable into a subject to be recollected and worked over in the mind." Like Freud's toddler, dramatizing his mother's departure and re-turn by flinging his toy out of sight and pulling it back again, Eliot could attempt to master her pain of loss by writing a story that would dramatize her mother's disappearance (the theft of Silas's gold and the death of Eppie's mother) as well as her return (the attachment between Silas and Eppie).

Eliot is also like Freud's "patient" who "cannot remember the whole of what is repressed" and "must *repeat* the re-pressed material as a contemporary experience." Through writing a work of fiction, Eliot could, like the patient in a therapeutic transference, enter into a fantasy in which she could reenact repressed feelings toward prior attachments. Through the interconnecting stories of her mirroring char-acters, Eppie and Silas (whose psychological situation is in turn mirrored by the leading characters in the Cass family subplot), the painful feelings that had previously been denied could be reconnected to the traumatic loss; thus the re-pressed pain could be confronted indirectly. When Silas re-turns to Lantern Yard to ask questions about his past, he comes to realize that some things would remain "dark"; sim-ilarly, in her own descent into what Mahler terms the "unre-memberable and unforgettable realm" of her mind, Eliot could not recover lost details of her infancy. She could, how-ever, repeat the process of losing and regaining her mother indirectly, through the writing of her fiction, as often as nec-essary to master her sense of loss. In the inspiration to write *Silas Marner*, her mind had thrust upon her a work of art that illuminates as it enacts its own progress toward self-healing.

Eliot's Identification with Eppie and Silas

Ruby V. Redinger

In the following article, Ruby V. Redinger discusses Eliot's writing of *Silas Marner* and her personal connection with Silas and Eppie. Redinger suggests that as a "weaver of tales" Eliot identifies with Silas, a weaver of linens. Furthermore, like Silas, Eliot was disconnected from society—in her case, due to her relationship with George Henry Lewes. Redinger also discusses the character of Eppie as a product of a possible fantasy of Eliot's dating back to her childhood—that of being a child separate or free from the ordinary family life. Ruby V. Redinger has written *The Golden Net* and edited the book, *Explorations in Living*. Her book on George Eliot is an important contribution to the psychology of Eliot and her writings.

It would seem that the specific idea for *Silas* did not come to George Eliot until a month after she had told Blackwood that she wished to write and publish an English novel before bringing out the Italian one. Under 28 November 1860, she entered in her Journal: "I am engaged now in writing a story, the idea of which came to me after our arrival in this house, and which has thrust itself between me and the other book I was meditating. It is 'Silas Marner, the Weaver of Raveloe.'" The "other book" may have been another English novel she was contemplating in order to fulfill her plan of publication but which had not taken a firm hold upon her; or it may have been what was to become *Romola*. We know that the Leweses had rented a house, 10 Harewood Square, furnished for six months, as all their efforts to find a suitable house to lease for a longer time had failed. The fact that she started *Silas* on 30 September, only five days after moving into the house, suggests that again living in London quickly

Excerpted from *George Eliot: The Emergent Self*, by Ruby V. Redinger. Copyright ©1975 by Ruby V. Redinger. Reprinted by permission of Alfred A. Knopf, a division of Random House, Inc.

forced into her mind the story of a man who had been alienated from his native society by an unjust accusation of theft, as well as by the perfidy of trusted friends. Everything she has to say about the conception of this story stresses the overwhelming power with which it invaded her mind and also the meager external detail upon which it was based. To [her publisher] Blackwood she wrote on 12 January 1861:

> I am writing a story which came *across* my other plans by a sudden inspiration. I don't know at present wether it will resolve itself into a book short enough for me to complete before Easter, or whether it will expand beyond that possibility. It seems to me that nobody will take any interest in it but myself, for it is extremely unlike the popular stories going; but Mr. Lewes declares that I am wrong, and says it is as good as anything I have done. It is a story of old-fashioned village life, which has unfolded itself from the merest millet-seed of thought.

Over a month later she had occasion to write again about the novel to Blackwood, who had by then read over half of it in manuscript form. Characteristically, he was admiring but sorry that the story so far lacked "brighter lights and some characters of whom one can think with pleasure as fellow creatures." He was also at this time skeptical of her prediction that the completed novel would take up only one volume; he had become familiar with her need to develop her characters and setting in a leisurely way that demanded space.

She wrote back on 24 February that she was quite certain about the length and that she was not surprised at his finding the story "rather sombre; indeed, I should not have believed that any one would have been interested in it but myself (since William Wordsworth is dead) if Mr. Lewes had not been strongly arrested by it." Actually, Lewes seems to have been less excited over *Silas* than any of her other novels, although he no doubt hoped that writing it would help restore her equilibrium after the devastating *Mill.* "I am in love with it," he wrote Blackwood when he sent more manuscript; but that is all he said. It is unlikely that Lewes went beyond the not very appealing Silas or the provincial life of Raveloe to the more abstract level of meaning intended by George Eliot. She admitted in her February letter to Blackwood that she had decided to subordinate this level to the realism:

> I have felt all through as if the story would have lent itself best to metrical rather than prose fiction, especially in all that relates to the psychology of Silas; except that, under that

treatment, there could not be an equal play of humour. It came to me first of all, quite suddenly, as a sort of legendary tale, suggested by my recollection of having once, in early childhood, seen a linen-weaver with a bag on his back; but, as my mind dwelt on the subject, I became inclined to a more realistic treatment.

Two weeks later she sent more manuscript and a motto from Wordsworth's *Michael* (lines 146-8):

A child, more than all other gifts
That earth can offer to declining man,
Brings hope with it, and forward-looking thoughts.

She was worried that this might indicate "the story too distinctly." When he had read the new manuscript, Blackwood was still in anxious search for happiness and upstanding character. He nonetheless wrote back reassuringly: "The motto giving to some extent the keynote to the story does not I think signify in this case, as whenever the child appears her mission is felt." Thus Blackwood was the first reader of *Silas* to recognize that Eppie—the child—was a force in the novel rather than a character.

When George Eliot had completed the novel and it was ready to appear in print, she answered [long-time friend] Charles Bray's inquiry about its nature by commenting once again on its origin: "It was quite a sudden inspiration that came across me in the midst of altogether different meditations." She was still thinking of this even after publication. In a conversation with Blackwood (who reported the talk to his wife), she gave a slightly changed version of the image which had provoked the inspiration: "'Silas Marner' sprang from her childish recollection of a man with a stoop and expression of face that led her to think that he was an alien from his fellows." In this later vision, the weaver's bag on his back—his burden—has been replaced by features suggesting alienation. As this is an improbable impression to have occurred to a child, it would seem that some force from her present life coincided with that vision from the past (the latter stayed intact to open the book). Thus it was the coming together of these two visions, each charged with its own meaning, which took the form of inspiration and demanded release, not at first as a realistic novel but as a poem and a legend. She checked her impulse toward poetic form, although in her own mind her material remained poetry. Yet the legend persisted in finding expression, perhaps to an extent of which she herself was unaware, for it came forth clothed in the illusion of realism which by now was second nature for her to create.

THE MYTHIC STRUCTURES OF *SILAS MARNER*

Silas Marner is her personal myth—a projection of an emotional pattern into a concise image that has the power to unfold into narrative. By mythic (although not realistic) identification, George Eliot, the weaver of tales, is Silas, the linen-weaver, who is unjustly ostracized by his native Lantern Yard. He makes his way to the town of Raveloe, which "lay in the rich central plain of what we are pleased to call Merry England . . . nestled in a snug, well-wooded hollow, quite an hour's journey on horseback from any turnpike, where it was never reached by the vibrations of the coach-horn or of public opinion" (Part I, chapter 1). Here he is tolerated, if not warmly welcomed, because of his craft ("the old linen-weaver in the neighbouring parish of Tarley being dead"), and also because of the superstitious fear aroused by his epilepsy, which, like idiocy, was thought to bring its possessor into touch with a source of truth closed to the normal individual. Had Silas not been an honest man, he might have played upon the awe of those who beheld his trances by "the subsequent creation of a vision in the form of resurgent memory; a less sane man might have believed in such a creation; but Silas was both sane and honest . . ." (Part I, chapter 1). In fact, it was a perfidious friend's taking advantage of this affliction that drove Silas out of Lantern Yard. But in Raveloe he was not persecuted because it was seen that he kept to himself and was harmlessly industrious: "he sought no man or woman, save for the purposes of his calling, or in order to supply himself with necessaries . . ." (Part I, chapter 1).

Having been falsely accused of theft at Lantern Yard, Silas becomes a miser at Raveloe, hoarding the golden guineas he rightfully earns from his painstaking labor. These are stolen from him, but eventually there appears a seemingly miraculous substitute—a girl-child whose hair is so much the color of the guineas that Silas at first thinks his gold has been restored to him. For a while, he is understandably dismayed by the child's presence. Then gradually she revives his stunted affections and trust, and it is through her that he regains total entry into society. This is the element of the myth contributed by the present. The transformation of

Silas's guineas into the child Eppie justifies George Eliot's seeking and accepting money for her writings because they have a humane value which is beyond measurement. Myths are timeless, so that this one is both a summation of the past and an adumbration of the future.

Myths are also fluid and metamorphic. In this one George Eliot is not only Silas; she is Eppie, who proves to be worth more than money and thus is some vindication of "such an unpromising woman-child"—as George Eliot described herself to Cara Bray [Charles's wife and another long-time friend] in October 1859, after the unexpected fame of *Adam Bede* had reached her but left her untouched because the triumph could not be enjoyed with her own family. Throughout her entire life at home, it seemed to her that her monetary value had been calculated with a shrewd eye. [Her older brother] Isaac had made it clear that in his opinion it was her intelligence which had led her into unorthodox ways of thinking and cut off her prospects of finding a husband. . . .

Coming perilously near the surface of the myth Eppie is also, even if only briefly, a sister. When Silas is at last convinced that what he has found on his hearth is not his guineas but a golden-haired child, a question darts across his mind: "Could this be his little sister come back to him in a dream—his little sister whom he had carried about in his arms for a year before she died, when he was a small boy without shoes or stockings?" The mere possibility that this might be so brought him "a vision of the old home and the old streets leading to Lantern Yard,—and within that vision another, of the thoughts which had been present with him in those far-off scenes." Unlike Isaac, and despite his isolation, Silas was still susceptible to the power of memory, which in him (as always in George Eliot) stirred feelings of love with a religious intensity. Led back to the past by thoughts of his sister, he felt the "old quiverings of tenderness,—old impressions of awe at the presentiment of some Power presiding over his life . . ." (Part I, chapter 12). Although soon forced to realize that the child is unknown to him, he reunites himself with his past by naming her Eppie, a shortened form of Hephzibah—the name of both his sister and his mother. Through Eppie he is reunited with his fellow men.

Yet another aspect of the myth has thus appeared, one which is unrelated in content but admirably suited for subtle incorporation into the Silas-Eppie relationship, although

Silas ceases to fulfill a significant role. As far as he knows, Eppie has appeared upon his hearth out of nowhere. Actually, having been attracted by the firelight from his cottage, the child had toddled right past him as he stood in a trance by his open door. Regaining his senses, he discovers her and gradually distinguishes her from both his money and his sister, finally accepting her as an unexplained message from his past life: "for his imagination had not yet extricated itself from the sense of mystery in the child's sudden presence, and had formed no conjectures of ordinary natural means by which the event could have been brought about" (Part I, chapter 12). This particular Eppie seems the product of a childhood fantasy which George Eliot had harbored for many years but which was only now coming to light as she worked through the strata of her mind in her writing. It is the not uncommon fantasy indulged in by highly inquisitive and imaginative children who sense their own birth as having been both miraculous and mysterious, so that they can dream freely about a destiny uncircumscribed by the known facts of an ordinary family background. In the narration of the novel, Eppie counters this part of the myth by spurning her revealed identity as the daughter of a wealthy man; but the abortive handling of this mythical element was necessitated by the fact that in a more important portion of the total myth, Eppie is already a symbol that has a value far greater than money. The myth concerning origin was to persist in George Eliot's novels: there is something of it in the story of Esther Lyon in *Felix Holt*; it operates on a grand scale in *The Spanish Gypsy*; and it is a constructive factor in leading Daniel Deronda to his special destiny, which is the founding of a new nation.

But these elements appear to be separate myths in *Silas* only when analyzed. Undergirding the narrative, they function as a single and continuous entity from which radiates an energy not seriously disturbed by the rational explanations given for the key symbols—Silas, Money, Eppie. It is this remarkably harmonious cooperation between myth and realism which gives rise to the balance and unity that pervade the novel and which has led to its being frequently dramatized and pictorially represented. The same reasons, as well as its convenient length, made it seem the ideal "literary" novel to be thrust upon young students. As a sad, but not surprising, result *Silas Marner* now rivals *The Spanish Gypsy* as George Eliot's least-read novel.

Literary Relationships and Affinities

Rosemary Ashton

Rosemary Ashton explores the various thematic issues that Eliot portrays in *Silas Marner.* Some of these issues include loss, redemption, and salvation. Moreover, Ashton relates these themes to Eliot's literary interests, including Eliot's affinities with William Wordsworth's Romantic philosophy, Coleridge's legendary Ancient Mariner, and other works of the seventeenth and eighteenth century. This article, which is an excerpt from Ashton's biography of George Eliot, also explores how Eliot's own life influenced her writing of *Silas Marner* and what the critical responses to the book were at the time of its publication. Rosemary Ashton is a professor of English literature at University College London. She has edited several editions of George Eliot's books. Ashton has also written several books on Victorian writers and other aspects of English literature.

[George Eliot] finished *Silas Marner* on 10 March [1861], six months after the idea had suggested itself to her. The novel is remarkable for its successful marriage of realism and romance, the historical and the legendary, for the exquisite blend of humour and pathos, and for its structural tautness. Being less than half the length of her first two novels, it lacks their large cast of characters, and their expansiveness of speech and narrative. What it lacks in scope, however, it makes up for in intensity and close patterning.

THEMATIC STRANDS FOUND IN *SILAS MARNER*

The plot is single, though it consists of the mirrored destinies of two men, Silas Marner, the lonely weaver, and Godfrey Cass, the son of the local squire. Silas is restored to life and

Excerpted from *George Eliot: A Life*, by Rosemary Ashton. Copyright ©1996 by Rosemary Ashton. Reprinted with permission from Penguin Books, UK.

love by finding and caring for the golden-haired child Eppie
on the spot where he used to keep his gold coins; Godfrey
self-interestedly denies his relationship to Eppie, and thereby
unwittingly dooms himself to a life of fatherlessness. Of
course it is the author who acts as providence, or Nemesis, by
making Godfrey childless in his marriage to Nancy, whom
he had feared to lose if he divulged his previous marriage to
Eppie's unfortunate mother. But we accept the patterning of
poetic justice, as we accept imaginatively George Eliot's plot
exploitation of superstition about weavers, ghosts, and the
mysterious, seemingly agentless, theft of Silas's gold without
giving intellectual assent to such superstition.

Here is a finely told tale illustrating that Nemesis . . . , but
in this case, as she promised Blackwood [her publisher] in
February 1861, the Nemesis is 'a very mild one'. Godfrey
Cass suffers in due proportion to his act of moral cowardice,
but his ending is not tragic. As he says ruefully to his faith-
ful wife, 'I wanted to pass for childless once, Nancy—I shall
pass for childless now against my wish.' The other strand of
the story, Silas's, is touching and in the end happy, illustrating, as George Eliot also told Blackwood, 'the remedial influences of pure, natural human relations'.

Wordsworth, whose spirit lurked in *The Mill on the Floss,*
particularly in the childhood scenes and in the narrator's
reverential comments about the influence of our early life
on later feelings and actions, is directly invoked in *Silas
Marner.* The novel is prefaced by three lines from Wordsworth's pastoral poem from the second edition of *Lyrical
Ballads,* 'Michael' (1800):

> A child, more than all other gifts
> That earth can offer to declining man,
> Brings hope with it, and forward-looking thoughts.

The ageing shepherd Michael, who fathers a child late in
life, finds his daily life and work renewed—

> from the Boy there came
> Feelings and emanations—things which were
> Light to the sun and music to the wind;
> . . . the old Man's heart seemed born again.

So it is with Silas Marner. The embittered exile from the
community makes a natural movement of nurturing towards the toddler who finds her way into his cottage, and by
awakening memories of a past he had blocked out, she returns him to humanity. George Eliot writes concisely but

movingly, as she does throughout this wonderful short novel. She exploits the fact of the weaver's shortsightedness by turning the arrival of Eppie—how she got there by crawling away from her opium-dosed and dying mother we know, though Silas does not—into a natural miracle:

Turning towards the hearth, where the two logs had fallen apart, and sent forth only a red uncertain glimmer, he seated himself on his fireside chair, and was stooping to push his logs together, when, to his blurred vision, it seemed as if there were gold on the floor in front of the hearth. Gold!—his own gold—brought back to him as mysteriously as it had been taken away! He felt his heart begin to beat violently, and for a few moments he was unable to stretch out his hand and grasp the restored treasure. The heap of gold seemed to glow and get larger beneath his agitated gaze. He leaned forward at last, and stretched forth his hand; but instead of hard coin with the familiar resisting outline, his fingers encountered soft warm curls. In utter amazement, Silas fell on his knees and bent his head low to examine the marvel: it was a sleeping child—a round, fair thing with soft yellow rings all over its head.

Eppie reminds him of his little sister, of his old home, long left behind under the bitterness of a false suspicion of theft. He now finds himself open to 'a hurrying influx of memories'. The child

stirred fibres that had never been moved in Raveloe—old quiverings of tenderness—old impressions of awe at the presentiment of some Power presiding over his life; for his imagination had not yet extricated itself from the sense of mystery in the child's sudden presence, and had formed no conjectures of ordinary natural means by which the event could have been brought about.

It *is* a mystery, a chance occurrence, but it is also natural and explicable. Here, if anywhere, George Eliot embodies her interest in, and insight into, the mystery that lies under the process of life she had invoked on reading Darwin's *Origin of Species*.

The story of Silas's bringing up of Eppie is beautifully told. As [Eliot's lover George Henry] Lewes assured Blackwood, who was afraid there would be too much sadness in the last third of the novel, what was to come was 'almost all pure sunshine & poetry'. In the spirit of 'Michael', George Eliot shows Eppie creating 'fresh and fresh links between his life and the lives from which he had hitherto shrunk continually into narrower isolation'. She needs his attention, and he needs—and is offered on all sides—help from his neighbours; she 'warmed him into joy because she had joy'. . . . Wordsworthian restoration of joy through a child and through closeness to nature, and the equally Wordsworthian notion of gain for loss (Eppie for gold) work unobtrusively through the story.

LITERARY AFFINITIES WITH *SILAS MARNER*

The realistic lower-class country setting of sixty years ago blends perfectly with the 'legendary tale' which George Eliot always spoke of as coming to her as an inspiration, prompted, appropriately, by memory. She told Blackwood in February that the idea came to her quite suddenly, 'suggested by my recollection of having once, *in early childhood,* seen a linen-weaver with a bag on his back' (my italics). Her shrewd reader Henry Crabb Robinson noticed, as he avidly read the novel in the Athenaeum Club when it came out, that not only was it Wordsworthian, but it had an affinity with Coleridge's 'Ancient Mariner' too. On reaching the point where Silas finds Eppie and refuses to let anyone else have her, he wrote, 'And he too will be saved, I see; it is to him what the blessing of the animals [i.e. the water-snakes] is to the Ancient Mariner.'

Robinson hit on something here, for George Eliot's novel seems poised between the complementary modes of Wordsworth and Coleridge as explained by the latter in his account of the origin of their joint volume of *Lyrical Ballads* (1798 and 1800) in chapter 14 of his *Biographia Literaria* (1817). Famously, Coleridge declared that his own aim had been to take 'persons and characters supernatural, or at least romantic' and bestow on them 'a human interest and a semblance of truth sufficient to procure for these shadows of imagination that willing suspension of disbelief for the moment, which constitutes poetic faith'. Wordsworth's task had been to 'give the charm of novelty to things of every day, and to excite a feeling analogous to the supernatural, by awakening the mind's attention from the lethargy of custom, and directing it to the loveliness and the wonders of the world before us'.

Silas Marner shares with the Ancient Mariner an almost legendary quality, and the things which happen to him are incomprehensible to him and seem symbolic and romantic to us; with Michael he shares an ordinariness, and sorrows and blessings which have an everyday source and existence while partaking of the mysterious, the archetypal, and the sacramental. 'Natural Supernaturalism', a phrase used by Carlyle in *Sartor Resartus* (1836), the book which Marian had so admired as a young woman, comes to mind too as appropriate to the ethos of *Silas Marner.*

Other legendary echoes and parallels are with *Pilgrim's Progress*, the story of the Prodigal Son (on which 'Michael' also draws), [Shakespeare's] *The Winter's Tale* with its sixteen-year gap and discovery of the lost daughter Perdita, and the fairy tale *Cinderella*, though in this case inverted, since Eppie refuses to be raised from her lowly status to that of 'princess' when Godfrey belatedly seeks to adopt the daughter he had once denied. The accent on family life, disrupted and disintegrated for Silas when he is a young man, and restored to him in middle and old age, also carries interesting modulated echoes of George Eliot's own experience of love lost and denied, exile from the family, and love found in another place in middle age.

The one aspect about Marian's life with Lewes about which no evidence remains, as far as I know, is how much, if at all, she regretted that her anomalous position dictated childlessness for her. We should be cautious about equating her feelings directly with those expressed with reference to any one of her characters, After all, like Shakespeare . . . she could think herself into the skin, and under it, of a wide variety of human types and individuals of either sex. Still, one's attention is drawn to a sentence describing the 'one main thread of painful experience' running through the married life of Godfrey Cass's wife Nancy, a woman happy with her husband but unhappy in her childlessness:

> This excessive rumination and self-questioning is perhaps a morbid habit inevitable to a mind of much moral sensibility when shut out from its due share of outward activity and of practical claims on its affections—inevitable to a noble-hearted, childless woman, when her lot is narrow. 'I can do so little—have I done it well?' is the perpetually recurring thought; and there are no voices calling her away from that soliloquy, no peremptory demands to divert energy from vain regret or superfluous scruple.

The one great difference between Nancy and the woman who wrote so understandingly about her situation is the very fact of the creative genius which made such writing possible.

CRITICAL RESPONSES TO *SILAS MARNER*

George Eliot finished writing *Silas Marner* on 10 March 1861, and it was published on 2 April. She and Lewes were preparing to take flight once more to Florence, where Marian wanted to continue the research for *Romola* which *Silas Marner* had interrupted. On 19 April they set off, leaving [Lewes's oldest son] Charles in charge of the house, but not of Pug, who had been lost a few months before. Blackwood kept them informed of the novel's sales. 7,500 copies were printed in the first month; by the end of the year something over 8,000 had been sold in one volume at 12/—, bringing George Eliot £1,600.

The critical response was quietly favourable. All the reviewers praised the verisimilitude and humour of the scenes at the Rainbow Inn, particularly in chapter 6, where the assembled villagers discuss their everyday concerns until interrupted by the exciting news of the theft of Silas's gold. Dallas in *The Times* once more saluted the charm and truth to life of George Eliot's writing. Richard Holt Hutton declared in the *Economist* that 'the conception is as fine as the execution is marvellous', and likened the Rainbow Inn chapters to the public house scenes in Shakespeare's *Henry IV* plays. Blackwood had written: 'You paint so naturally that in your hands the veriest earthworms become most interesting perfect studies in fact.' And perhaps most gratifying of all, Thornie [Lewes's younger son] wrote from Edinburgh that he enjoyed the novel so much that when he reached the last page, he 'almost got angry at there being no more of it'.

Inasmuch as Marian could feel relaxed and content about any of her works, she could feel so about *Silas Marner*. It was produced with less despair than any of its predecessors or successors; its publication was attended with no unpleasant feelings between her and Blackwood; there was no Liggins to worry about; and none of the critics invoked the vision of the author as a strong-minded woman of dubious morals. This was due, no doubt, partly to the lack of opportunity afforded by the story for scandalized comment about gynaecological handbooks and sexual errors, and partly to the fact that readers and critics were becoming used to the difficult idea that a woman with unconventional religious views and unconventional domestic arrangements could write novel upon novel full of sympathy, humour, and genius.

Eliot's Views on Motherhood in *Silas Marner*

Rosemarie Bodenheimer

In this excerpt from her book, Rosemarie Bodenheimer discusses George Eliot's relationship with
George Henry Lewes's oldest sons and how it relates
to her portrayal of parenthood in *Silas Marner*.
Bodenheimer concentrates on Eliot's views on
motherhood as found in her own life and the lives
of her friends. These relationships are what form
Eliot's representation of families, in particular
motherless families, in *Silas Marner*. Rosemarie
Bodenheimer is a professor of English at Boston College. She has published several articles on Victorian
literature and authors, including *The Politics of Story
in Victorian Social Fiction* and *The Real Life of Mary
Ann Evans: George Eliot, Her Letters and Fiction*.

The experience of 1860 confronted Marian Lewes [the name
Eliot adopted when she lived with George Henry Lewes]
with several kinds of self-division. In "adopting" Charles
[Lewes's oldest son] and sacrificing her health and spirits for
the sake of his development, she was proving to herself and
her correspondents that she was as responsive as any other
woman to the Victorian morality of motherhood. The idea of
Lewes's children solidified her status as "Mrs. Lewes," as
she was at pains to point out to a correspondent who had
called her Miss Evans: "For the last six years I have ceased
to be 'Miss Evans' for any one who has personal relations
with me—having held myself under all the responsibilities
of a married woman. I wish this to be distinctly understood;
and when I tell you that we have a great boy of eighteen at
home who calls me 'mother,' as well as two other boys, almost as tall, who write to me under the same name, you will

understand that the point is not one of mere egoism or personal dignity, when I request that any one who has a regard for me will cease to speak of me by my maiden name." The name of "mother" reinforces the fiction of "Mrs. Lewes," which in turn protects the purity of adolescent children; thus Marian, bolstering her anomalous position, calls upon her correspondent's own sensitivity to the taboos that protect family life. At the same time, however, she was exquisitely aware that her relationship with Charles would have to be invented through patient domestic work, and conscious that she relied heavily on the work of other substitute parents to allay her guilt about the care and teaching of Thornton and Herbert. Her hope that Charles might help to normalize her status in the community contended against her suppressed resentment at the drain on resources of time, energy, mental freedom, and money which the boys represented. It was at this moment that the idea for *Silas Marner* "thrust itself" upon her.

The idea for the story "came to me after our arrival in this house, and . . . thrust itself between me and the other book I was meditating," Marian noted in her journal during the November spent at Harewood Square. The internally resisted move to Harewood Square had been made on September 24; three days later Thornie [Lewes's second son] had arrived for his three-day sojourn. Immediately after he left, George Eliot began *Silas Marner.* "The other book" was of course *Romola,* which had been conceived during the Italian journey, but *Marner* seems also to have displaced an undisclosed plan for "another English story" mentioned to Blackwood in an August letter. Split as it is between the stories of a successfully adopted girl baby and the maimed fortunes of the Cass brothers, *Silas Marner* incorporates and transforms many of Marian Lewes's immediate maternal concerns.

MOTHERHOOD IN *SILAS MARNER*

The linked double plot of the fable is a subtle vehicle for an oblique rendering of the simultaneous gain and loss of motherhood which Marian experienced in her early forties. The magical story of Silas and Eppie isolates the wishful elements: social redemption by adoptive parenthood, and the desire for a beautiful, unformed girl child with no remembered history that might separate her from a perfect connection with her parent. The story of the Cass brothers and

Nancy Lammeter dramatizes experienced anxieties and res-
ignations: the unmothered Cass boys threaten to waste their
lives along with their father's money, and their murky history is morally connected to Nancy Lammeter's brave but
saddened childlessness. The perfection that many readers
experience in reading this fable testifies to the extraordinary
coalescence of old images and new emotions which allowed
George Eliot to write so directly, and so indirectly, of a current preoccupation. Her successful transformation of family
concerns into the stuff of fabular history might be measured
by the fact that Thornton Lewes was one of the tale's most
ardent admirers.

The ways in which George Eliot projects herself in Silas
Marner are manifold and have often been told. Both are
weavers and wanderers, known for their cleverness, wear-
ing a faint air of incipient criminality, falsely accused of
stealing and unable to answer their accusers, separated and
outcast from a severely religious past, living internal lives
completely at odds with the prevailing opinions about them.
Yet the identification with an alienated hoarder was also one
of the oldest self-images in Mary Ann Evans's vocabulary. It
appears in a religious poem written at the age of nineteen, in
which the speaker casts off all beloved earthly things in a series of stanzas, each ending in "Farewell!" Of the ten stanzas,
only one speaks an original image:

> Books that have been to me as chests of gold.
> Which, miser like, I secretly have told,
> And for them love, health, friendship, peace have sold,
>   Farewell!

The series of metaphorical displacements, from the secret
life with books to the literal hoarding of gold to the golden
hair of the miraculously appearing child, indicates that the
image of hoarded gold had always signified a guiltily un-
shared wealth of antisocial life rather than the accumulation
of money itself. Silas's own love of his guineas has to do with
the companionship of their familiar "faces" rather than with
their purchasing power; he thinks of his half-earned guineas
"as if they had been unborn children" that allow his imagination to move into the future (chap. 2). When Eppie's human face is substituted for the guineas, he is still reluctant to
share her, and the successive stages of his resocialization
are marked by the necessity of doing so. Only in this way
does the story mildly suggest the old conflict activated when

Marian Lewes began to share her husband and household with his son.

For the most part the Silas-Eppie story is a fairy tale of substitute parenthood which derives its appeal from its understanding of impossible wishes. The transfer of Eppie from her mother to her new forty-year-old father is performed when both adults are unconscious; it is naturalized by the erasure of choice. Silas's weaving is interrupted by Eppie's needs, creating no tension but the anxiety of perfect love. Discipline is abandoned, but Eppie grows up perfectly anyway, "the burden of her misdeeds being borne vicariously by her father Silas" (chap. 14). The narrative repeatedly insists that Eppie reconnects Silas with his forgotten past, and especially with his mother and dead little sister, after whom Eppie is named; in fact, Silas is transformed into a maternal figure himself. By the end of their story Lantern Yard, the scene of Silas's betrayal, is literally wiped off the landscape.

SUBSTITUTE FAMILIES

It is the Lantern Yard story, however, which shadows forth the possibility that substitute families might be as cruel as natural ones. The relation between William Dane and Silas Marner parallels that of the Cass brothers; in both cases the "evil brother" steals from the father figure (in Lantern Yard the senior deacon, a childless widower) in a way that inculpates the innocent and muzzled brother. The figure of a young man sneaking off with the parental bags of gold—here as in "Brother Jacob," and again revised [in her novel *Romola*] in Tito Melema's sale of his foster father's rings—seems to have been a powerful one in George Eliot's imagination at this time.

In the story of the Cass brothers the image is grounded in the absence of the loving mother's discipline. Without this "fountain of wholesome love and fear" (chap. 3), without "the sweet flower of courtesy" (chap. 9), the Cass sons, "kept home in idleness," have "turned out rather ill" (chap. 3). Nancy Lammeter's little provincial codes of household order do not prevent her from being a redemptive maternal force in the Cass manor; Godfrey, the son who yearns for domesticity, is made good by his marriage to her. In the second part of the fable, when Godfrey is said to be about forty, the narrative turns, for the first and only time in George Eliot's fiction, to examine the conjunction of a successful womanly redemption with the fact of childlessness. Both the emptiness of Nancy's lot and the parental yearning of Godfrey's are occasions for the production of sentences that demonstrate the clarity with which George Eliot could formulate, master, and exempt herself from the stresses of her own emotional life. Of Nancy the narrator says, "This excessive rumination and self-questioning is perhaps a morbid habit inevitable to a mind of much moral sensibility when shut out from its due share of outward activity and of practical claims on its affections—inevitable to a noblehearted, childless woman, when her lot is narrow" (chap. 17). Of Godfrey's continual fretting after a child: "I suppose it is the way with all men and women who reach middle age without the clear perception that life never *can* be thoroughly joyous: under the vague dullness of the grey hours, dissatisfaction seeks a definite object, and finds it in the privation of an untried good. Dissatisfaction, seated musingly on a childless hearth, thinks with envy of the fattier whose return is greeted by young voices—seated at the meal where the little heads rise one above another like nursery plants, it sees a black care hovering behind every one of them, and thinks the impulses by which men abandon freedom, and seek for ties, are surely nothing but a brief madness" (chap. 17). From her double position as childless woman and anxious parent, she understood both kinds of fantasy.

THE BRAY FAMILY

In sketching the story of the Cass attempt to reclaim Eppie as Godfrey's natural daughter, George Eliot was aided by a model less intimate than her own. In 1846 Charles and Cara Bray [Eliot's long-time friends], themselves childless, had adopted Bray's natural daughter Elinor, born to his longtime mistress. Nelly Bray lived with the family from infancy until the age of nineteen, when she died of pulmonary consumption, tended lovingly by Cara and Sara Hennell. In her twenties, then, Marian Evans had become familiar with a situation that offered the burdens and satisfactions of motherhood to two very close friends; when she later "inherited" Lewes's children she began writing to Cara and Sara with a greater sense of equality in the matter of stepmotherhood. ("I used to feel your elevation above me continually in the attitude of mind you showed about Nelly's education and your sense of your relation towards childhood generally," she wrote to Sara in July 1864, when Nelly's illness had become acute). The story of Nancy Lammeter, whose superstitious belief forbids her from meddling with Providence by choosing to adopt a child but who believes that the father by blood has a greater claim than any foster father, may be derived in some way from the experience of Cara Bray. Yet Nancy—unlike Cara and like Marian Lewes—is deprived of the opportunity to bring up an infant; the question of adoption is raised only when Eppie is eighteen and devoted to Silas Marner, and Nancy, having once resigned herself to childlessness, must resign herself over again to the knowledge that she might have had Eppie as a baby if Godfrey had been honest with her. It is in the presence of her forgiving but unrelentingly noncompensatory vision that the wedding which ends *Silas Marner* is most property celebrated.

During the months when George Eliot was imagining how Eppie and Nancy rehumanize and redeem male households, Marian Lewes worked at loving and domesticating Charles. In a mood of New Year's assessment, she wrote to Blackwood on January 1, 1861, "I suppose I shall never love London, or believe that I am as well in the streets as in the fields . . . but the duty of staying in it, has a counterbalancing pleasure when one has a great boy, who is learning to love home better than anything outside it." The new "family trio" may have recalled the old days of life with another father and son, Robert and Isaac Evans; it is possible that Marian's frequently expressed gratitude about Charles's temperament was underscored by memories of stress in the earlier family triangle.

Aspects of Eliot's Life Are Reflected in the Themes of *Silas Marner*

Frederick R. Karl

In this essay, Frederick R. Karl combines biographical and thematic issues in a discussion of the novel and its writing. Thus, while taking a chronological approach to Eliot's writing, Karl also integrates a discussion of her psychological state and how that influenced *Silas Marner*'s themes and issues. Frederick R. Karl is the author of several books on authors, including biographies of Franz Kafka, William Faulkner, and Joseph Conrad. This essay is an excerpt from his biography on George Eliot.

With the move to [her new home at] Blandford Square [Eliot] could look forward to three years of relative quiet, and a sudden burst of energy on *Silas Marner*—thirteen chapters would be sent to [her publisher] Blackwood on 15 February—indicates how rapidly she could turn herself around. But even that burst of energy could not disguise the fact that she felt low and feeble, caught in a depressive cycle. So forceful are her complaints that even Blackwood, not usually given to personal intervention, expressed concern. He counsels her that she needs exercise.

ELIOT'S LIFE IN 1860

Silas Marner, a book which probes profoundly into shadows of its author's own life, finally surfaces. "I am writing a story," she says, "which came *across* my other plans by a sudden inspiration. I don't know at present whether it will resolve itself into a book short enough for me to complete before Easter. . . . it seems to me that nobody will take any interest in it but myself, for it is extremely unlike the popular stories going. . . ." [Her lover George Henry] Lewes, how-

Excerpted from *George Eliot: Voice of a Century, a Biography,* by Frederick R. Karl. Copyright ©1995 by Frederick R. Karl. Reprinted by permission of W.W. Norton & Co., Inc.

ever, said it was as good as anything she had done, just the reinforcement she required.

Silas Marner did not come by "a sudden inspiration." It was a natural progression, embodying in imagined episodes and characters qualities intimately wedded to Eliot herself. Marner's obsession with money is not to be neglected as Eliot and Lewes build up their fortune, including piles of investments, nor is the sudden appearance of a child who saves Marner to be disengaged from the appearance of Charles in Eliot's life. Further, Marner's basic marginality and isolation—his solitary work at his loom, his social estrangement—are not to be ignored in the light of Eliot's own profession at her desk and her own disinclination for social life and fear of scandal. Money dooms, even as one devours it; and the love of a child saves. Work itself is, also, salvational: lonely work, without anyone intruding or criticizing.

Eliot confessed she felt "timid" in her writing, and perhaps that was the result of her worry about houses and servants and the boys. With her energy sapped, she nevertheless hoped her new quiet might bring fictional renewal. *Silas Marner* was written in and around just this sense of living in a trough. Another source of company was Lewes's mother, Mrs. John Willim, who, while she remained on good terms with Agnes, was proud of her son's second wife. She and Eliot met for the first time in 1860, and then when the couple moved to Blandford Square near the end of that year, they were close enough for her to visit. Her complaints were legion, most of them related to her eighty-six-year-old irritating husband, Captain Willim, whom she often threatened to leave. At one point, Lewes said she could live with them, although we do not know Eliot's opinion about this. The irony was that while Lewes's mother was admiring of her daughter-in-law's fame (and riches, one should add), Eliot's own family remained not only distant but silent.

The portrait Samuel Laurence made of her at this time, in 1860, is pensive, quite sad—as opposed to the more forceful Mayall/Rajon etching, a retouched photograph. The 1860 drawing does bear out Eliot's own dismal assessment of herself, so undefined is the face, despite the dominant long nose. Her lips are not expressive, and there is no hint of animation. Part of the taste in drawing then was based on pre-Raphaelite painting and drawing, which emphasized the pensive, faraway look. Eliot surely has that—she stares into the distance, without clear focus or definition, or even interest. What is so striking about her oval face, pensive eyes, long nose, hair parted in the middle and falling artlessly is the lack of definition such a powerhouse of a person projects. All the tensions and divisions remained securely hidden, part of a secret self.

ELIOT'S LIFE IN 1861

The month of January (1861) proved so unrelentingly grim that she and Lewes decided to flee the city for the country. With Charles, they went to Dorking, twenty miles south of London, in Surrey, for an overnight, and then themselves stayed on in the area until Tuesday. The fresh air appeared to energize her, for, as noted, she enjoyed a long pull on *Silas Marner.*

In a completely different area, that of political life, as we survey Eliot's responses in early 1861, we notice she has passed through several years in the 1850s with virtually no comment on the Crimean War or on other issues of the day. Except for a brief notice of the ratification of the English-Russian peace treaty of 1856, her letters and journal indicate no involvement in that larger world, or no desire to set down her thoughts. The Crimean War, in particular, should have created some interest, especially since Lewes and Eliot knew people close to Florence Nightingale; but even in its own right, the war brought forth serious political realignments in southeastern Europe and changed the course of England's political relationship with Russia. England's other movements into North Africa, into central and South Africa, its intermittent wars with Zulus in the south and with Muslims in the north, and its campaigns in India and Afghanistan are all missing from Eliot's correspondence. There is almost no mention of the government, except, perhaps, her note that Queen Victoria was reading *Mill.* The change of prime ministers, the advent of Disraeli (whom she distrusted), his challenge by Gladstone, and the deep policy splits this represented do not appear to have engaged her thought. It is all the more strange because Lewes was himself interested in a broad range of subjects, and their conversation must have taken up political and social ideas. Further, their friend Herbert Spencer was deeply immersed in social issues, and not only theoretically.

There are several explanations, one being that the couple

had so turned in on themselves, creating an island impenetrable by the rest of the world, that their isolated state excluded that larger world. Even when Eliot did respond to political life, as in *Felix Holt, the Radical,* and then *Middlemarch,* her focus is localized; whatever national issues are involved are subsumed in a local election. Larger questions of policy and political ideology are marginalized. This leads us to another explanation, that because Eliot wrote so intimately about personal history and related beliefs, projected imaginatively into her fiction, she consciously excluded anything she could not experience directly. Her distinctive voice derived from her assimilation of all policy questions into moral behavior, into ethical decisions, the sole things that counted for her.

On 15 February, she sent Blackwood 230 pages of manuscript, about 100 pages under what she estimated would be the final length of *Silas Marner.* She was hurrying along as she wanted an Easter publication—Easter Sunday was 31 March, and *Marner* appeared two days later. Blackwood's response to the first 100 pages was admiring, although he wished the "picture had been a more cheery one and embraced higher specimens of humanity," but, he added, "you paint so naturally that in your hands the veriest earthworms become most interesting perfect studies in fact." He sees the child, Eppie, as restoring Marner to a more Christian frame of mind. He comments further that his sole objection is the absence of "brighter lights and some characters of whom one can think with pleasure as fellow creatures. . . ." He looks forward to this in the remainder of the manuscript. The question then becomes whether he should offer one volume at 12 shillings or two smaller volumes. He assures her, in a remark that makes the contemporary reader breathless, that he can put the whole into type in a very few days.

Eliot agreed it should be one volume, and then tried to explain the tale's somberness. She says Nemesis is very mild here, and the entire purpose of the story is heuristic, to reveal the "remedial influence of pure, natural human relations." She adds: "it came to me first of all, quite suddenly, as a sort of legendary tale, suggested by my recollection of having once, in early childhood, seen a linen-weaver with a bag on his back; but, as my mind dwelt on the subject, I became inclined to a more realistic treatment." She says she wants to publish the story now because she likes her works to appear in the order she wrote them, since they represent successive mental phases. "Brother Jacob," not published until 1864, was an exception.

In response, Blackwood offered generous terms of £800 for an edition of 4,000 copies, payable six months from publication, and a like payment for any copies sold beyond the 4,000. He hoped to sell 5,000–6,000 copies, although the library sale might be smaller than expected because of one-volume (as against three-decker) publication. He was sanguine that would be offset by private purchasers, willing to put out 12 shillings for one volume, whereas they would not spend over a pound and a half for three.

Eliot accepted the terms and asked for an advertisement saying "New Work by George Eliot," and the novel to be called *Silas Marner, the Weaver of Raveloe*. By 4 March, Eliot sent on more manuscript, seeing the end in about thirty pages. Her motto for the title page derives from Wordsworth's poem "Michael": "A child more than all other gifts/That earth can offer to declining man,/Brings hope with it, and forward-looking thoughts." By 10 March, final pages were delivered to the firm. *Marner* emerged as if Eliot had been programmed for it. Lewes told Blackwood he was occasionally made anxious (his word) by her belittling of what she writes. We may assume that only by perceiving her writing as triumphing over her disabilities—ill health, perception of failure, inability to achieve her ideals—could she produce the writing itself. It was a product of a poor self-image, which she could transform into the strength of the word, in some kind of transmutation of self into language. It was a workable arrangement. . . .

BIOGRAPHICAL SIMILARITIES BETWEEN ELIOT AND MARNER

Specific biographical similarities between Eliot and Marner are even more compelling than general ones. In one respect, Eliot was interested in regeneration of a lost soul, or in the restoration of spiritual life in someone who had focused exclusively on hard, unyielding matter. In another respect, she was eager to castigate the squirearchy for its dissolution, its thievery, its lack of moral principle, its failure even to recognize its own daughter. By this means, she could laud the working class, who appear as honest, hardworking, and focused. In a third way, she was attempting to reveal how guilt must eventually be confronted: that the really evil are punished—Dunstan in drowning, Molly in freezing during an opium stupor—while Godfrey is saved by facing the truth. In a fourth respect, she was interested in textures themselves: soft versus hard, gullible versus strident, the warmth of the cottage hearth versus the coolness of the large house on the hill. In still a further respect—and here we have the engine that drives the novel—Eliot used the material as a personal myth, as the myth of Marian Evans/Mrs. Lewes/George Eliot: what she believed, both consciously and unconsciously, and how she could emerge in the question of a theft.

The accumulation and then theft of Marner's money has certain intimate overtones for the author. The "theft" does seem linked to Eliot's uncertainty about her work, her inability to listen to even the slightest criticism, her sense of her writing as falling beneath the highest achievement, and her more generalized fear that everything was precarious. The theft, to this extent, is linked to deep inner anxieties that it all might vanish, that something—destiny, circumstance, Nemesis—was waiting to dispossess her of her gifts, and it would all be swallowed up as rapidly as it appeared. This is not too different from the lifting of the veil, in that story, which leads to disillusionment, not clarification.

That could be one area of theft which parallels Marner's loss of his treasure trove, but perhaps not the major one. A more central view would be that Eliot saw herself as part of a "theft." She had "stolen" Agnes's husband; she was the thieving receiver of someone else's children, Lewes's boys; she had stolen a particular kind of life in the face of social opprobrium. This view depends on how deeply Eliot confronted her position and how much credibility she gave to it. But if we read her remarks and asides correctly, we know she felt profoundly distressed about her social ostracism and isolation and had developed several defenses to protect herself. Her perception is of someone who has stolen what clearly does not belong to her.

Related to theft is guilt and, not distant from that, the "myth" of Eliot, of a person sinking, shaping, and reshaping. Money—the hoard, the treasure, the mystique of a kind of power—is the "other" which provides a false sense of security or an artificial self. Also not far off is sibling rivalry, which by *Silas Marner* had become a constant in her work—here deadly in its implications. Many of these relationships, as in *Marner*, contain disturbing elements, from mere rivalry to

outright hostility and hatred. Intertwined with all in this novel
is a not unrelated reaction, guilt.

MONETARY ISSUES

The fact that this novel is not major Eliot does not lessen the
biographical weight. For guilt here is part of the condemnation of money at just the time Eliot and Lewes were becoming particularly greedy about building a fortune, or creating
a treasure trove, well beyond their personal needs. The condemnation does not take the form of a Marxist or other social critique of money but is based solidly on a Christian
view of Jesus driving the moneylenders from the temple
and by so doing condemning the accumulation of a hoard.
The classical myths of a warrior chasing after a treasure—
Jason and the golden fleece, and others—are brought into
play in Marner's humble cottage, and there subjected to a
Christian critique. The play of elements in Eliot is compelling: the idea of a treasure as a compensation for past in-
justices; an absorption in the hard but dead matter of coins,
the fascination with the golden glitter; the character's social
withdrawal and isolation while the hoard accumulates; the
compensatory life which comes, essentially, from fingering
dead matter, the despair and depression implicit in this
solitary act; the sexual connotations of this lonely activity,
the manipulation of piles of coins, of arrangement, the need
to keep touching so as to create a "reality"; the perversion
implied here, of an unconscious drive to accumulate power
even as one's actual position loses it; the perverse act of
writing itself, the self-absorption and even narcissism
translated into money, whether in piles of glittering coins or
in securities and bank accounts.

Much of the activity occurs at the hearth in Marner's cottage—with the hearth taking on its classical role as a holy
place where the gods of hearth and home (the Roman Lares
and Penates) are honored for their protection. Here Marner
fingers and counts his money; here he compensates for the
loss of money with the child Eppie; and here he redeems
himself as a social being. That Eliot has cast the novel back
in the early part of the century, and before that for Marner's
expulsion from Lantern Yard, is fitting. Also fitting is her
use of the Eden myth: the expulsion, the entrance into a
wasteland of sorts, the gradual accommodation to the world
beyond the Garden, a world full of conspiracy and criminal

activity. Within such contexts—the past, the sacred hearth, an innocent child—Marner can transform himself from a falsely accused guilty person and from a bizarre, solitary, almost lunatic-like weaver into someone who can give and receive love.

Since the child Eppie is compensatory for Marner's monetary loss, we must move back into Eliot's shadowy, unconscious response to her position. As she approached her forty-second year, she recognized the impossibility of childbearing; Eliot, in fact, told a friend that she and Lewes decided not to have children and took precautions. By this time, she may well have been menopausal, in itself a difficult time psychologically for a woman without her own children. But her growing desire to acquire money cannot be discounted as compensatory—in *her* perception—for her failure to fulfill traditional wife and mother roles. Tellingly, Marner becomes as much a mother to Eppie as a father; and, pointedly, the child is female, so that he must assume more of the maternal role than with a male child. In a gender switchover, he serves as father in his earning capacity as a weaver, but as traditional mother in his way of raising Eppie to be a fine young woman. Also, not to be discounted in the equation is Eliot's new role as stepmother—a maternal role she had to balance with her own "work," not at the loom, but at her desk.

Her hortatory, moralistic tone has increased considerably over her previous work. Money, so desirable, has become an evil force. But more than money is involved in this internal struggle for which moral advice seems a palliative. . . .

Not disconnected to the above internal struggle shaping up was Eliot's artistic effort to make *Marner* more than realistic without forsaking realism. She adopted several strategies. Marner's "gaze" suggests a mystery, not only demonic but otherworldly, as though his head and his body moved in separate directions. He also suffers an epileptic fit during a prayer meeting, which associates him with devil worship. Raveloe is itself somewhat shrouded, "a village where many of the old echoes lingered, undrowned by new voices." Once in Raveloe, where Marner has arrived in the 1780s, he experiences reveries, part of that "other world" he inhabits. He is described, at his loom, as a spider, a "spinning insect," suggesting his linkage to the natural, rather than human, world. Then in his association with treasure, he takes on the mythical connotations of the keeper of the hoard, like Alberich in the Wagner Ring cycle. And when he emerges into the light—that is, when his life is illuminated by Eppie—he assumes a certain Christ-like quality.

All of this heightens Eliot's supra-realism even while allowing her to maintain, nevertheless, a strong social realism: the townspeople and the tavern scenes, and subsidiary figures like Godfrey and Dunstan Cass, old Squire Cass, Nancy Lammeter (a Lucy Deane figure), the peasant Dolly Winthrop, the doomed Molly, and others. This part is consistent with *Silas Marner*'s Wordsworthian qualities: the unity of people and nonhuman elements is evident. Woods, hearth, quarry, plants, flowers, and seasons are all continuous with human activity, and underscore the interwoven quality of the lives and their environment. Marner weaves, and Eliot encloses him in one woven web after another, nearly all of them connected to lower-class or working-class life. It is fitting that Marner's adopted daughter should marry a gardener. Nowhere else has Eliot tried so determinedly to dramatize the drab life of people for whom startling events are almost unknown, even as these lives push against an "unreal" or mysterious world. . . .

PUBLICATION OF *SILAS MARNER*

The couple's return to Blandford Square coincided with the book's appearance, the first reviews, and the death of Major William Blackwood, on 8 April. The reviews were admiring, especially the one in the *Saturday Review* (13 April), whose critic located Eliot in the company of Dickens and Bulwer-Lytton, even Scott, and saw her as possibly superior. Lewes probably read out parts of this to Eliot. The *Economist* (27 April) lauded both book and author. The important review in the *Times*, by E.S. Dallas, was an author's dream, equal to the one in the *Saturday Review.* "To George Eliot," Dallas begins, "belongs this praise—that not only is every one of her tales a masterpiece, but also they may be opened at almost any page, and the eye is certain to light upon something worth reading. . . ." And it ends: "The moral purpose which is evident in her writings is mostly an unconscious purpose. It is that sort of moral meaning which belongs to every great work of art. . . ."

Even the *Westminster Review*, which had savaged much of *Mill*, came around, calling *Marner* her finest, although this may have been left-handed praise. The following year, the reviewer in the *Dublin University Magazine*, as if in some Irish vendetta against British literature, continued with the Eliot bashing that had begun with *Mill*. Withal, Eliot was fortunate in her reviews, for while *Marner* does have its telling aspects, it is small beer among her other fictions—an interlude with strong personal baggage, but a limited perspective.

She and Lewes were now trying to arrange their affairs and prepare for another long trip, a return to Italy and to Florence in particular. Possibly, a large check from Blackwood, for £1,350, on 1 April, helped them decide to go at this time; the monies derived from additional sales of *Mill* starting with the fifth thousand copy. Eliot said she was grateful for the money as protection against the time when she was no longer able to write well. The decision having been made to leave on 19 April, she wrote Samuel Laurence that she did not wish to have his portrait of her exhibited at the Royal Academy; in fact, she wanted the portrait kept within his own studio. In time, Laurence sold it to Blackwood's, where it was framed and hung in the book room of the London office. Amidst this, Eliot found time to comfort John Blackwood in several letters for the death of his brother, although she herself had not been deeply attached to the major.

CHAPTER 2

Major Themes

Alienation in *Silas Marner*

Fred C. Thomson

Fred C. Thomson explores the theme of alienation in the novel, particularly how Silas is originally isolated from his society but later becomes reintegrated into it. Thomson initially discusses Silas's precarious social position in the community of Lantern Yard but speaks more at length about the transformation from outcast to member of society in Raveloe. By exploring the evolution of this theme in the novel, Thomson illustrates how *Silas Marner* relates to Eliot's other works and exemplifies the tragic forces in Eliot's writings. Fred C. Thomson is a professor who has written many articles and books on English literature. He has done quite a bit of work on George Eliot's novel, *Felix Holt*. Recently he edited a new edition of *Felix Holt* for Oxford's World Classics.

Silas Marner, though gradually being rehabilitated from its dreadful fate as a required "classic" for adolescents, is nevertheless still to the rear in due appreciation among the novels of George Eliot. *Middlemarch* continues to command the bulk of critical attention, and no doubt rightly. It is an imaginative achievement of a very high order, but this should not prevent wider recognition of the specific contributions toward its creation by its slighter predecessor.

Silas Marner in the Context of Eliot's Other Works

The tendency is to regard *Silas Marner* as something of an exception in George Eliot's fiction. While admiring her customary merits of stylistic control, deft characterization, and sensitive realistic evocation of provincial England, commentators have generally located the distinctive quality of the book in its formal perfection, "fairy tale" simplicity, and

Excerpted from "The Theme of Alienation in *Silas Marner*," by Fred C. Thomson, *Nineteenth-Century Fiction*, June 1965. Copyright ©1965 by The Regents of the University of California. Reprinted with permission from The University of California Press.

overt, almost systematic symbolism—qualities they find less conspicuous in the bigger novels. They have looked upon it, in other words, as a delightful branch or inlet rather than as part of the mainstream of George Eliot's art. Yet the contention here will be that *Silas Marner* does in fact belong to that mainstream, and in particular is important to the development of the author's vision of tragic life, so impressively projected in *Middlemarch.*

Not that *Silas Marner* is a tragedy. Certainly the main contour of the second half and the ending are of an opposite nature; but the portions describing Silas' exile, loneliness, and deprivation are dark-hued indeed. One feels that at least in these pages George Eliot was experimenting with a tragic mode. In a letter to [her publisher] John Blackwood she said, "I have felt all through as if the story would have lent itself best to metrical rather than prose fiction, especially in all that relates to the psychology of Silas; except that, under that treatment, there could not be an equal play of humour." Though in some of her shorter poems George Eliot did essay humor, the implication in this context is that poetry might have heightened the tragic aspect of Silas' plight. As it is, the first two chapters have a sustained somber tonality oddly different from almost anything in her previous novels.

Take, for example, *The Mill on the Floss,* published a year before *Silas Marner.* It too, if hardly a thorough-going tragedy, has definite tragic colorations. On the whole, however, it conforms to the traditional "comic" or optimistic orientation of the English novel, with the underlying predication of a stable world, wherein the individual is placed in coherent relationship to his society. Whatever the flaws in that society, the fundamental values by which it exists are never seriously questioned. Maggie inhabits a relatively integrated world in which she may be an insurgent but not an alien. At times confused and rebellious in her hazy aspirations for a better life, she is always presented as a *member* of her society, whether in its favor or disfavor. She acknowledges its authority and does not dispute its right to punish her. . . .

To convey a more genuinely tragic vision of life, George Eliot had to suggest vaster, less easily discernible or accessible sanctions and powers than Maggie's conscience or the petty tyranny of St. Ogg's society. She had to find a way of portraying characters ill-attuned to the ruling conditions of the world, a way of putting more inscrutability into the operation of human destinies. This mysteriousness need not be entirely cosmic; it could also suffuse intricate social relationships. It must, however, be handled otherwise than in *The Mill on the Floss.*

REALISM AND THE SUPERNATURAL

The opening paragraph of *Silas Marner* indicates one possible, if severely limited, direction in its neat balance of realism and quasi-supernaturalism:

> In the days when the spinning-wheels hummed busily in the farmhouses—and even great ladies, clothed in silk and threadlace, had their toy spinning-wheels of polished oak—there might be seen, in districts far away among the lanes, or deep in the bosom of the hills, certain pallid undersized men, who, by the side of the brawny country-folk, looked like the remnants of a disinherited race. The shepherd's dog barked fiercely when one of these alien-looking men appeared on the upland, dark against the early winter sunset; for what dog likes a figure bent under a heavy bag?—and these pale men rarely stirred abroad without that mysterious burden. The shepherd himself, though he had good reason to believe that the bag held nothing but flaxen thread, or else the long rolls of strong linen spun from that thread, was not quite sure that this trade of weaving, indispensable though it was, could be carried on entirely without the help of the Evil One.

George Eliot commences by setting the story in a vaguely distant past, but simultaneously qualifies any aura of strangeness by associating the age with a practical domestic activity. Within this temporal frame, she moves from the sheltered farmhouses and upper-class estates to the exposed outskirts of civilization, where the occasional wanderers of as yet unspecified occupation are seen in sharp contrast to the natives. Their comparison with the "remnants of a disinherited race" bears mysterious allusive connotations, but the structure of the simile suggests that they are really not such Ahasuerian exiles. Moreover, in the context of the sentence, they would seem to have some connection with spinning. Intimations of the occult aroused by the dog's barking at the silhouette against a wintry sunset are dispelled by the prosaic interpretation. The focus next shifts to the shepherd's apprehensions about the figure and his mysterious bag, and again the rational explanation is offered, the grounds for any supernatural reality being transferred to rustic superstition.

Such devices are not particularly original and contribute

only superficially to the story's tragic substance. They help generate a preparatory mood, but do not in themselves provide the conditions for a tragic world. The local peasantry may feel awe and mystery, but George Eliot as narrator plainly repudiates any share in their crude superstitions. From sentence four to the end of the paragraph, she delivers a little treatise on vulgar errors that lays the blame squarely on ignorance and insularity.

In that far-off time superstition clung easily round every person or thing that was at all unwonted, or even intermittent and occasional merely, like the visits of the pedlar or the knife-grinder. No one knew where wandering men had their homes or their origin; and how was a man to be explained unless you at least knew somebody who knew his father and mother? To the peasants of old times, the world outside their own direct experience was a region of vagueness and mystery: to their untravelled thought a state of wandering was a conception as dim as the winter life of the swallows that came back with the spring; and even a settler, if he came from distant parts, hardly ever ceased to be viewed with a remnant of distrust, which would have prevented any surprise if a long course of inoffensive conduct on his part had ended in the commission of a crime; especially if he had any reputation for knowledge, or showed any skill in handicraft. All cleverness, whether in the rapid use of that difficult instrument the tongue, or in some other art unfamiliar to villagers, was in itself suspicious: honest folks, born and bred in a visible manner, were mostly not overwise or clever—at least, not beyond such a matter as knowing the signs of the weather; and the process by which rapidity and dexterity of any kind were acquired was so wholly hidden, that they partook of the nature of conjuring. In this way it came to pass that those scattered linen-weavers—emigrants from the town into the country—were to the last regarded as aliens by their rustic neighbours, and usually contracted the eccentric habits which belong to a state of loneliness.

But if George Eliot discredits supernatural mystery, she at the same time recognizes mystery of an intellectually more acceptable sort. In the sense of discontinuity or of disconnection she perceives a common experience with tragic possibilities on a level of actuality surpassing the comprehension of the unenlightened countryfolk. If the rustic mind was inclined to detect in discontinuity the external agency of the Evil One, she sees it rather as an illusion wrought by the circumstantial limits of knowledge and by the submerged internal processes of society. Beneath the slightly condescending irony of her rationalism in analysing peasant superstition, she insinuates a further irony, that in truth the world *is* mysterious. In more sophisticated societies, the boundaries of knowledge are extended and may be translated into terms other than geographical, but there persists the same wonder, so to speak, about "the winter life of the swallows," the same helplessness before the hidden yet humanly determinable origins of things and events. We seldom know enough that could be known at the moment when it would do most good. As George Eliot writes [in *Felix Holt*], "there is no private life which has not been determined by a wider public life, from the time when the primeval milkmaid had to wander with the wanderings of her clan because the cow she milked was one of a herd which had made the pastures bare."

THE TRAGIC FORCES IN *SILAS MARNER*

Tragic force in *Felix Holt* and *Middlemarch* seems to derive from a peculiar combination of spiritual and social alienation and the often obscure social interactions that nourish or intensify it. I have suggested that in *The Mill on the Floss* this combination was lacking. For all the range and depth of social observation, one misses the sense of *process,* the proliferous entanglement of circumstance that with the uncritical passes for Destiny, and that can wear down or destroy the individual who challenges its power. In *Silas Marner*, George Eliot succeeded in selecting and organizing precisely the ingredients required for her special concept of tragedy. Even though she developed her materials inversely toward a happy conclusion for Silas, the weaver is her first full study of alienation, anticipating the subtler, more complex treatments of the theme [in later novels].

She claimed that the genesis of the book was inspirational: "It came to me first of all, quite suddenly, as a sort of legendary tale, suggested by my recollection of having once, in early childhood seen a linen-weaver with a bag on his back. . . ." Not the least important feature of the germinal image is the fact that the solitary figure is a weaver. As such he plies a staple trade, one that the opening sentence stresses is identified with a closely ordered society. But the sentence also juxtaposes to the picture of a busy domestic and communal life a fragmentary glimpse of an unhoused, rootless, stunted, lonely breed of men, who are nevertheless connected with the same occupation as the feminine spinners. Society cannot get along without the weavers, nor could the weavers survive without a society to buy their products. Yet in rural areas the position of these weavers is anomalous. They are both indispensable and distrusted, the very bag containing the stuff for their looms increasing their suspiciousness in local eyes. Business is transacted with them almost as if in furtive pact with the Evil One. George Eliot has thus chosen a protagonist whose trade combines the familiar and the strange, whose way of life is both continuous and discontinuous with established society. The whole story is based upon a pattern of these dichotomies.

Silas is equipped with a history of alienation that reaches much further back than his arrival in Raveloe. His whole life has been a series of disconnections. An orphaned impoverished artisan pent in a squalid alley in the heart of a Northern industrial town, his opportunities for social participation have been restricted to a Dissenting sect splintered off by its narrow principles from both the religious Establishment and the surrounding secular world. Even within this tight brotherhood, Silas becomes separated from his fellows by the unaccountable fits, which he refuses to exploit to his advantage. His cramped beliefs, poor education, and ignorance of human nature, together with his natural capacities for affection and faith, conspire to make him preeminently vulnerable to the misfortunes that suddenly befall him. In devastating succession, he is bereft of friendship, fellowship, love, faith in divine justice, home, native town—everything, in fact, that had meaning for him. The disaster is especially radical because his loss is not so much material as spiritual. Silas must learn to live not only in an entirely different region but with an entirely new set of values, or rather with the shards of his old ones.

> In the early ages of the world, we know, it was believed that each territory was inhabited and ruled by its own divinities, so that a man could cross the bordering heights and be out of the reach of his native gods, whose presence was confined to the streams and the groves and the hills among which he had lived from his birth. And poor Silas was vaguely conscious of something not unlike the feeling of primitive men, when they fled thus, in fear or in sullenness, from the face of an unpropitious deity. It seemed to him that the Power in which he had vainly trusted among the streets and in the prayer-meetings, was very far away from this land in which he had taken refuge, where men lived in careless abundance, knowing and needing nothing of that trust, which, for him, had been turned to bitterness. The little light he possessed spread its

beams so narrowly, that frustrated belief was a curtain broad
enough to create for him the blackness of night.

Notice that George Eliot nowhere commits herself to belief
in the objective reality of any such superhuman Power (ma-
lign, benign, or neutral) as Silas feels has stricken him. The
causes of his ruin, she is careful to show, are all naturally
explicable, and the source of mystery is his contracted understanding. As Jerome Thale [in *The Novels of George Eliot*]
acutely puts it, "What he has lost is not a creed but a sense
of the world."

THE CONTRASTS BETWEEN LANTERN YARD AND RAVELOE

The contrasts between the religiously and secularly oriented
societies of Lantern Yard and Raveloe are explicitly drawn
near the start of chapter ii. Lantern Yard, "within sight of the
widespread hill-sides," is an interior, upward-yearning
world, physically enclosed by the white walls of the chapel,
yet boundless for spiritual aspiration. To Silas the immediate
palpable environment matters less than the sounds and
rhythms, the hymns and scripture, which by their familiarity have become the surrogates or guarantees of exalted un-
seen but devoutly trusted realities.

> The white-washed walls; the little pews where well-known
> figures entered with a subdued rustling, and where first one
> well-known voice and then another, pitched in a peculiar key
> of petition, uttered phrases at once occult and familiar, like
> the amulet worn on the heart; the pulpit where the minister
> delivered unquestioned doctrine, and swayed to and fro, and
> handled the book in a long accustomed manner; the very
> pauses between the couplets of the hymn, as it was given out,
> and the recurrent swell of voices in song: these things had
> been the channel of divine influences to Marner—they were
> the fostering home of his religious emotions—they were
> Christianity and God's kingdom upon earth.

Conversely, in low-lying, wood-screened Raveloe, the
church is an exterior to the lounging men, the tempo of life
relaxed and meandering, the satisfactions and realities de-
cidedly earthbound.

> And what could be more unlike that Lantern Yard world than
> the world in Raveloe?—orchards looking lazy with neglected
> plenty; the large church in the wide churchyard, which men
> gazed at lounging at their own doors in service-time; the
> purple-faced farmers jogging along the lanes or turning in at
> the Rainbow; homesteads, where men supped heavily and
> slept in the light of the evening hearth, and where women
> seemed to be laying up a stock of linen for the life to come.

These details are shrewdly calculated to penetrate the merely visual differentia of the two places and to reveal their intrinsic spiritual opposition.

With the advent of Silas in Raveloe, George Eliot has a thematic precursor of a central situation in *Middlemarch*—a person living with the wreckage or confusion of ardent spiritual ideals in a mediocre, spiritually atrophied society. The differences are, of course, many. Dorothea and Lydgate are in a manner trapped by their society, whereas Silas is virtually independent of Raveloe, living on its fringes and for years hardly affecting its consciousness. When he is finally reached by the community, it acts wholesomely upon him instead of oppressively. But these and other distinctions aside, the important thing is that George Eliot was here studying in simplified and diagrammatic form the mutual relationship of an indigenous society and an outsider. *Middlemarch* is a massive, highly complex variation on the theme of its pilot model. Of considerable interest, therefore, are the methods by which a sense of disjunction is communicated in *Silas Marner.*

The village itself is appropriately situated for its function. Nestled in the fertile Midlands and comfortably prosperous, it is still out of touch with the broader life of England and has long been sinking into torpid obsolescence. The simple, self-contained structure of this tiny society enables George Eliot to sketch its principal stratifications and interrelationships with spare economy and to polarize two units of roughly comparable narrative weight—a compact social organization and an alienated individual. At the outset, as I have indicated, George Eliot superimposes upon a background of ancient inert social stability an antithetical motif of transient deracination. She then descends from generalities to particulars, describing the superstitious speculations in Raveloe about the strange appearance and habits of Silas.

Noteworthy is the absence of the dialogue that fills the Cass episodes and the period of Silas' reclamation. During the first fifteen years of his stay in Raveloe, he is talked about rather than to; and the narrator effectively preserves this breach of communication by never letting the minds of Silas and the villagers join. To the latter, he remains a vaguely sinister enigma whose presence is taken for granted but whose inner character is opaque. For instance, the curing of Sally Oates is first alluded to as a matter for dark conjecture.

Later we get Silas' point of view and learn that his powers and motives have been sadly misconstrued. The abortive result of his benevolent impulse is to deepen the isolation from which he could then have been rescued. Likewise, his history might have brought him sympathy if told to a villager; but it is interpolated for the information of the reader, and sealed off from the knowledge of the community. Silas' eventual recital of it to Dolly Winthrop is an important milestone in his restoration to a unified existence.

SILAS' ALIENATION FROM SOCIETY

The disconnection of Silas from society is systematically expressed by contrasting groups of image and metaphor. Despite the bad farming, intellectual somnolence, coarse hedonism, and tacky gentry of Raveloe, the place does have a kind of weedy or overripe vitality, observable in the drowsy impressions, of laden orchards, nutty hedgerows, and thick woods. There is a human parallel in the clustered homesteads, cosy domesticity, heavy conviviality, and indolent pace of the natives. Silas, on the other hand, after the austere yet warm communal life in Lantern Yard, where the brethren enjoyed an emotional solidarity through song, worship, and doctrine, is associated with images of death and inorganic nature—withering vegetation, drying sap, the shrunken rivulet in barren sand, stone, iron, and of course the gold. His very appearance mirrors his abstraction from ordinary life: "Strangely Marner's face and figure shrank and bent themselves into a constant mechanical relation to the objects of his life, so that he produced the same sort of impression as a handle or a crooked tube, which has no meaning standing apart." Even the sound of his loom, "so unlike the natural cheerful trotting of the winnowing machine, or the simple rhythm of the flail," is a jarring note in the Raveloe world. After the fiasco with Sally Oates, he renounces his once-beloved excursions for herbs and diminishes to subhuman existence.

> Then there were the calls of hunger; and Silas, in his solitude, had to provide his own breakfast, dinner and supper, to fetch his own water from the well, and put his own kettle on the fire; and all these immediate promptings helped, along with the weaving, to reduce his life to the unquestioning activity of a spinning insect.

Besides indicating the insect level to which Silas has declined, the simile of the spider has a further significance related to the theme of social discontinuity. [Critic] Reva Stump has argued that the pervasive web imagery in *Middlemarch,* when related to the characters of Lydgate, Rosamond, Casaubon, and Bulstrode, is "connected with illusion and egoism rather than with reality and fellow-feeling." In a footnote, she adds that in *Silas Marner* this imagery "is used to point up the deficiency in Silas' vision. The insular world he creates can be entered only by the child, and she alone can lead him out of it." This interpretation can perhaps be a little amplified, for the web image in *Silas Marner* happens to be both metaphorical and objective. Silas is an actual professional weaver, but since his disaster his work at the loom has become for him a sterile abstraction instead of a useful social function. For him it serves no purpose except to feed his own unhealthy obsessions. In this respect, he recalls [Jonathan] Swift's spider in the Apologue, who, alone in his fortress, spun out of excrement and venom in poisonous "self-sufficiency." Preoccupation with the abstract geometry of the woven cloth leads to the absurd fascination with the geometry of the multiplying piles of gold. Silas is not even linked economically to Raveloe by the money it pays him, because the value of the coins for him does not lie in their negotiability. They are taken out of circulation, and thus with each gold piece the weaver recedes further from contact with human society and meaningful reality. This perversion of values is suggested by an ironic metaphor of organic growth:

> But now, when all purpose was gone, that habit of looking towards the money and grasping it with a sense of fulfilled effort made a loam that was deep enough for the seeds of desire; and as Silas walked homeward across the fields in the twilight, he drew out the money, and thought it was brighter in the gathering gloom.

SILAS' REINTEGRATION WITH SOCIETY

The second half of the book deals with Silas' regeneration, showing how his life is rewoven with society and how his work once again acquires a purpose other than as a deadening refuge from despair; and as this occurs, the imagery of sunlight and gardens irradiates and vitalizes the scenes. The elaborate metaphorical substructures of the later novels, which so enrich their tragic dimensions, surely owe something to the experimentation with similar but more exposed techniques in *Silas Marner.*

The recurrent fits, in addition to making Silas an object of suspicion and aversion, represent chasms of consciousness which permit the seemingly gratuitous intrusion of evil or good. On two widely separated occasions, they mark an apparent disconnection from the past and a resumed continuity, respectively. Silas feels in these involuntary suspensions the manifestations of some controlling Power. Though aware that William Dane has wrongly and maliciously accused him of theft, he regards himself the victim of divine as well as human betrayal. That brief lapse of consciousness breaks for him absolutely the continuity of past and present, and the shock is worsened by his essentially emotional reaction.

> To people accustomed to reason about the forms in which their religious feeling has incorporated itself, it is difficult to enter into that simple, untaught state of mind in which the form and the feeling have never been severed by an act of reflection. We are apt to think it inevitable that a man in Marner's position should have begun to question the validity of an appeal to the divine judgment by drawing lots; but to him this would have been an effort of independent thought such as he had never known; and he must have made the effort at a moment when all his energies were turned into the anguish of disappointed faith.

He is unable to make a rational response to the experience and to seek out a new basis for coherence in his shattered beliefs. Flight to Raveloe completes this vacuum of existence. "Minds that have been unhinged from their old faith and love, have perhaps sought this Lethean influence of exile, in which the past becomes dreamy because its symbols have all vanished, and the present too is dreamy because it is linked with no memories."

The effect on Silas of his second crucial seizure, during which Eppie crawls into the cottage, is different but also dependent upon an emotional response. The sight of the child curiously revives old memories of a happier time, casting a frail lifeline of hope back to the past. From then on, the texture of his life is rewoven, and he comes to recognize that the great rift between past and present had existed more in his embittered imagination than in reality. There is much that he still cannot understand, but he can again have trust in a benevolent unity to the world. After Dolly Winthrop's eloquently inarticulate musings on Providential design, he replies,

> Nay, nay, . . . you're i' the right, Mrs Winthrop—you're i' the

right. There's good i' this world—I've a feeling o' that now; and it makes a man feel as there's a good more no he can see, i' spite o' the trouble and the wickedness. That drawing o' the lots is dark; but the child was sent to me: there's dealings with us—there's dealings.

So the two fits at the beginning and end of Silas' desperate years signify a superficial discontinuity of experience that masks a deeper actual continuity, individual and collective.

Interestingly, Dunstan Cass does not steal the gold while Silas is in a trance, as might easily have been arranged. Instead, George Eliot devises a painstaking account of why Silas was absent from home and the door unlocked. It is arguable that she was relieving the excess of coincidence a little, but in a semi-legendary tale of this sort, coincidence is not very bothersome. A better explanation, I think, is that at this moment Silas and the society of Raveloe begin at last to converge. More specifically, the destinies of Silas and the Cass family intermesh and subsequently operate upon one another in remarkable ways. During the crucial fits, Silas is the *passive* recipient of bad fortune and good, whereas in this intermediate crisis he is conscious and *active*. The episode illustrates the far-reaching web of social interaction that often produces baffling consequences—"that mutual influence of dissimilar destinies," as George Eliot once phrased it. While Silas has been in the village at an unwonted hour, Dunstan has been in the cottage for the only time in his life and without any prior acquaintance with the weaver. The result is a mystery with incalculable repercussions. For Silas, the discovery of his loss brings greater desolation and discontinuity than ever. He does not realize that the catastrophe is really salvation. Injury to him by a Cass is soon followed by a compensatory "gift" from a Cass. George Eliot emphasizes that because of Silas' altered habits since the robbery Eppie gets into the cottage instead of freezing to death outside. The deadly gold is replaced by the living child, the sight of whom reunites Silas with the past. The how and why of all this, so mysterious to the weaver, has its rationale in the affairs of certain people hitherto total strangers to him.

THE DOUBLE PLOT OF *SILAS MARNER*

It is a commonplace that the double plot in *Silas Marner* was something of an innovation for George Eliot, but it has not been sufficiently noted that this feature plus the alienated character comprise the basic tragic ingredients of her later novels. . . . If the outcome for Silas is serene, under other circumstances it could well have been wretched. The point is that the double plot is used less for the sake of variety, parallelism, or contrast than to explore the actual workings of society, especially the minute reticulation of influences.

At the time of the theft, the quality and values of Raveloe are represented by the Casses. The Squire is the "greatest man" around and sets the standard for the good life with his abundant feasts. But in his pursuit of pleasure he neglects husbandry and the farm is slipping toward ruin, temporarily averted by the precarious bounty of wartime prices. Furthermore, since the death of his wife the house has become rundown and gloomy; his sons are quarreling amongst themselves and going to the bad. The real social center of Raveloe is thus not Red House but the Rainbow, a status confirmed by the frequent patronage of the Squire himself. And it is to the Rainbow that Silas runs for help after the theft. The effect of that visit is to enlist the sympathy of the villagers, "beery or bungling" as their demonstrations of it may be. At any rate, not only does Silas begin to be drawn into the community but his troubles, like those of Wordsworth's Cumberland Beggar, kindle some feeble glow in the mouldering better natures of the rustics. However, the influence of Silas upon any general elevation of the quality of Raveloe life should not be exaggerated. The major reciprocal influences are between Silas and Godfrey Cass.

Silas' second errand for aid is on behalf of another person, and he goes to the domestic center of Raveloe, Red House (itself a kind of "rainbow" with its Blue Room and White Parlour). He there touches momentarily the world of Godfrey Cass, whose daughter becomes his savior. Godfrey in deciding *not* to acknowledge the child and to leave her in the keeping of Silas helps the weaver to renewed life; but he also changes the course of his own life. He reforms, marries the efficient Nancy Lammeter, and restores the farm to stable prosperity. Red House, and in fact the whole village, seem to recover a bloom that had turned sere in the early chapters. Offsetting these benefits, Godfrey remains childless, unable to transmit his new affluence through a direct heir. And as a consequence of his expanding economy, the pit is drained, disclosing Dunstan's skeleton and the gold. The family has long been bound to Silas by a secret debt—a debt which

Godfrey now finds must be repaid not merely with the gold but with the loss of his child and the probable extinction of his line. Silas has been to him both a benefactor and an unwitting Nemesis.

Thus by combining the theme of social and spiritual discontinuity with the double plot, George Eliot approached a means of expressing her concept of tragic life. Instead of referring to some cosmic or metaphysical source for the sense of mysterious power, she implanted it in the organism of society itself. Tragedy occurs when the well-intentioned individual acts in ignorance or defiance of the intricate web that binds his moral behavior to that of the collective society; and the resultant tragic *experience* consists in the feeling of disconnection from the roots of one's beliefs and assumptions about what the world is like. Silas is therefore a tragic figure insofar as his narrow piety prevents an adequate response to the patent injustice done him, and insofar as his response *is* a feeling of utter alienation. In *Silas Marner*, the relationship of individual discontinuity and social continuity is examined in rather too schematic or didactic fashion. It all works a little too slickly to pass for objective reality. But in *Felix Holt*, still experimentally and with uneven success, and in *Middlemarch*, triumphantly, George Eliot mastered the techniques and language introduced in her "legendary tale."

The Theme of Rebirth and Redemption

Walter Allen

In this article, Walter Allen discusses the theme of
spiritual rebirth, tracing events from Lantern Yard
through Silas's gradual recovery in the village of
Raveloe. In the first part of the article, Allen traces
Silas's spiritual journey by concentrating on the folk
wisdom and character of the village itself, noting
how the villagers help Silas rediscover his moral
core by embracing him into their fellowship. In the
second part of the article, Allen discusses the differences between the villagers and the gentry of Raveloe, emphasizing the character of Dolly Winthrop,
whom Allen terms a "positively good person" who
embodies the folk wisdom of Raveloe and the "truth
of feeling." Walter Allen has written several books on
English literature. This article is from his book entitled, *George Eliot.* Other books include *The English
Novel: A Short Critical History* and *The Modern
Novel in Britain and the United States.*

George Eliot wrote *Silas Marner, the Weaver of Raveloe* between November, 1860, and March, 1861; it "has thrust itself
between me and the other book I was meditating" (*Romola*).

Though slight, *Silas Marner* is as perfect a work of prose
fiction as any in the language, a small miracle. It is a book
that in her own time only George Eliot could have brought
off and that, since her day, no English or American novelist
would have dared attempt. She herself described its especial
quality, writing to her publisher Blackwood, as well as anyone has ever done:

> I don't wonder at your finding my story, as far as you have
> read it, rather sombre: indeed, I should not have believed that
> anyone would have been interested in it but myself (since
> Wordsworth is dead) if Mr. Lewes had not been strongly ar-

Excerpted from *George Eliot,* by Walter Allen (New York: Macmillan, 1965).

rested by it. But I hope you will not find it at all a sad story, as it whole, since it sets—or is intended to set—in a strong light the remedial influences of pure, natural human relations. The Nemesis is a very mild one. I have felt all through as if the story would have lent itself best to metrical rather than to prose fiction, especially in all that relates to the psychology of Silas; except that, under that treatment, there could not be an equal play of humour. It came to me first quite suddenly, as a sort of legendary tale, suggested by my recollection of having once, in early childhood, seen a linen weaver with a bag on his back; but as my mind dwelt on the subject, I became inclined to a more realistic treatment.

Fortunately, George Eliot did not attempt to write *Silas Marner* in verse, for, though she wrote two volumes of verse, she was no poet; all that are still remembered of her verses are the lines, in Wordsworthian blank verse, from *O May I Join the Choir Invisible,* which were much anthologised during the nineteenth century, and the sonnet sequence *Brother and Sister*—and that for its possible autobiographical connotations rather than for its quality as poetry. . . .

THE SETTING OF *SILAS MARNER*

And though, as she began to write [*Silas Marner*], she gave her story "a more realistic treatment," it remains a "sort of legendary tale." Indeed, the note of legend, of events occurring in a past already remote, is struck in the very first sentence of the story: "In the days when the spinning wheels hummed busily in the farmhouses—and even great ladies, clothed in silk and thread lace, had their toy spinning wheels of polished oak—there might be seen, in districts far away among the lanes, or deep in the bosom of the hills, certain pallid undersized men who, by the side of the brawny countryfolk, looked like the remnants of a disinherited race."

So strong is the evocation of remoteness, even of something like the timelessness of fairyland, that it comes as a shock to realise that the action narrated took place in a generation that ended within only a few years of the author's own birth. The events described are not dated with any exactitude, but they cover about thirty years on the very eve of the Victorian age. Yet, even so, they belong, and did when George Eliot was writing the story, to a period as irretrievably in the past as Shakespeare's England.

What had happened, of course, was the coming of the railway. As a modern historian has said: "When the Duke of Wellington attended the opening of the new Manchester and

Liverpool Railway in September, 1830, he witnessed an event as important in its own way as the Battle of Waterloo, which he had won fifteen years before. It symbolised the conquest of space and parochialism." It took the Industrial Revolution everywhere; it meant the disappearance of villages like Raveloe, the tempo of whose existence had remained almost unchanged for centuries. The "districts far away among the lanes, or deep in the bosom of the hills" were far away no longer but wide open to the influence of the great world. By 1860, the story of Silas Marner would have been impossible, for the very naïvety of the characters—villagers, gentry and Marner alike—and their rusticity would have been impossible.

It is this naïvety, this rusticity, along with the remoteness of the time and the place, that gives *Silas Marner* its charm. The remoteness also made it possible for George Eliot to tell a story of the utmost simplicity.

THE REBIRTH OF SILAS MARNER

Silas Marner is essentially a myth of spiritual rebirth. Marner, the Methodist weaver, pallid, undersized, a child of the dark, satanic mills of the Industrial Revolution, loses his faith when he is accused of and found guilty by his fellow-Methodists of a particularly mean theft. Almost crazed by despair, he leaves the town and wanders through the country, finally settling on the edge of a village worlds away from the Industrial Revolution, unaffected by it, and therefore worlds away from life as he has known it.

The difference between Raveloe and the town of his origins is so great, indeed, as to make communication between him and his new neighbours all but impossible. To the villagers, it did not seem certain that "this trade of weaving, indispensable though it was, could be carried on entirely without the help of the Evil One." The sound of Silas's loom, not far from the edge of a deserted stone pit, is "questionable" and has "a half-fearful fascination for the Raveloe boys." His gaze was "enough to make them take to their legs in terror. For how was it possible for them to believe that those large brown protuberant eyes in Silas Marner's pale face really saw nothing very distinctly that was not close to them, and not rather that their dreadful stare could dart cramp, or rickets, or a wry mouth at any boy who happened to be in the rear?" Unwittingly, Marner is caught in the "strange lingering echoes of the old demon worship" of the villagers. His very strangeness makes him an object of superstitious fear, and for want of an alternative, he becomes a miser. Then, mysteriously, he is robbed of his hoard of gold, which in due time is, as it were, magically replaced by a golden-haired baby girl whom he finds on his hearth. To the child, Eppie, he devotes himself as ardently as before to his gold. It is as though the precious metal has been transmuted into human affection, and one result of this is that he is accepted without question by the community of Raveloe.

This is plainly of the stuff of myth, and when the followers of [psychologist and theorist Carl] Jung discover *Silas Marner,* they will have a field day. We are in the presence of the magical; but the magical is mediated for us by the superstition of the villagers, for whom magic is still a reality.

Silas Marner's affinities to the fairy-tale are obvious enough, but it is a fairy-tale saturated in the sense of the actual. It is this that gives it its enduring power to compel belief. There is Raveloe itself:

. . . orchards looking lazy with neglected plenty; the large church in the wide churchyard, which men gazed at lounging at their own doors in service time; the purple-faced farmers jogging along the lanes or turning in at the Rainbow; homesteads, where men supped heavily and slept in the light of the evening hearth, and where women seemed to be laying up a stock of linen for the life to come.

It exists in sharp contrast to the industrial world of Lantern Yard, from which Marner has emerged. "In the early ages of the world, we know, it was believed that each territory was inhabited and ruled by its own divinities, so that a man could cross the bordering heights and be out of reach of his native gods, whose presence was confined to the streams and the groves and the hills among which he had lived from his birth." The author's comment indicates the primitive quality of life in Raveloe, which is self-contained and self-sufficient. To it, in a curious way throughout the book, Marner is marginal. He is the character who must convince us—the villagers are there in all their actuality, palpable creatures of flesh and blood and rich idiosyncratic speech; but George Eliot handles Marner with consummate skill.

His presence broods over the novel, but his appearances in it are anything but continuous; he is, in fact, off-stage more often than he is on. We see him with a double vision: as the lost, crazed, pathetic being George Eliot presents and also as the mysterious stranger he is to the villagers. But it is the villagers who are the norm of life in the novel; they are created with great warmth and affection, and when they take Marner into their fellowship, we accept him also.

THE VILLAGERS AND COMMUNITY IN RAVELOE

In a sense—beautifully differentiated from one another though the villagers are—Raveloe is itself a character in the novel, a corporate entity, as it were, with its own personality. Part of it is indicated in the following:

> The inhabitants of Raveloe were not severely regular in their church-going, and perhaps there was hardly a person in the parish who would not have held that to go to church every Sunday in the calendar would have shown a greedy desire to stand well with Heaven, and get an undue advantage over their neighbours—a wish to be better than the "common run" that would have implied a reflection on those who had had godfathers and godmothers as well as themselves, and had an equal right to the burying-service.

The entity that is Raveloe has its wisdom; but it is a folk-wisdom, a lore inherited from time immemorial, the expression of a way of life that has scarcely changed over generations. The villagers speak, as it were, in chorus, antiphonally, as in the wonderful scenes in the Rainbow Inn and the interchanges between Mr. Macey and Mr. Winthrop, Mr. Tookey, the butcher and the farrier and Mr. Snell, the landlord, scenes that take us back to Shakespeare's comic rustics and anticipate Hardy's:

> "Come, come," said the landlord; "let the cow alone. The truth lies atween you: you're both right and both wrong, as I always say. And as for the cow's being Mr. Lammeter's, I say nothing to that; but this I say, as the Rainbow's the Rainbow. And for the matter o' that, if the talk is to be o' the Lammeters, *you* know the most o' that head, eh, Mr. Macey? You remember when first Mr. Lammeter's father come into these parts, and took the Warrens?"

> Mr. Macey, tailor and parish clerk, the latter of which functions rheumatism had of late obliged him to share with a small-featured young man who sat opposite him, held his white head on one side, and twirled his thumbs with an air of complacency, slightly seasoned with criticism. He smiled pityingly, in answer to the landlord's appeal, and said:

> "Ay, ay; I know; but I let other folks talk. I've laid by now, and gev up to the young uns. Ask them as have been to school at Tarley: they've learnt pernouncing; that's come up since my day."

"If you're pointing at me, Mr. Macey," said the deputy clerk, with an air of anxious propriety, "I'm nowise a man to speak out of my place. As the psalm says:

'I know what's right, nor only so,
But also practice what I know.'"

"Well, then, I wish you'd keep hold o' the tune when it's set for you; if you're for prac*tis*ing, I wish you'd prac*tise* that," said a large, jocose-looking man, an excellent wheelwright in his weekday capacity, but on Sundays leader of the choir. He winked, as he spoke, at two of the company, who were known officially as the "bassoon" and the "key bugle," in the confidence that he was expressing the sense of the musical profession in Raveloe.

Mr. Tookey, the deputy clerk, who shared the unpopularity common to deputies, turned very red, but replied, with careful moderation, "Mr. Winthrop, if you'll bring me any proof as I'm in the wrong, I'm not the man to say I won't alter. But there's people set up their own ears for a standard, and expect the whole choir to follow 'em. There may be two opinions, I hope."

"Ay, ay," said Mr. Macey, who felt very well satisfied with this attack on youthful presumption; "you're right there, Tookey: there's always two 'pinions; there's the 'pinion a man has of hissen, and there's the 'pinion other folks have on him. There'd be two 'pinions about a cracked bell, if the bell could hear itself,"

"Well, Mr. Macey," said poor Tookey, serious amidst the general laughter, "I undertook to partially fill up the office of parish clerk by Mr. Crackenthorp's desire, whenever your infirmities should make you unfitting; and it's one of the rights thereof to sing in the choir—else why have you done same yourself?"

"Ah, but the old gentleman and you are two folks," said Ben Winthrop. "The old gentleman's got a gift. Why, the Squire used to invite him to take a glass, only to hear him sing 'The Red Rover'; didn't he, Mr. Macey? It's a natural gift. There's my little lad Aaron, he's got a gift—he can sing a tune straight off—like a throstle. But as for you, Master Tookey, you'd better stick to your 'Amens': your voice is well enough when you keep it up your nose. It's your inside as isn't right made for music: it's no better nor a hollow stalk."

In Raveloe the right opinion is the opinion other people have, the community opinion. But there is something else to be noted about the community that is Raveloe: it speaks with one voice, one accent. This comes out in the speech of the chorus of ladies preparing for the dance at the Red House, in Chapter 11, which in its way balances the male chorus at the Rainbow:

"Don't talk *so*," said Nancy, blushing. "You know I don't mean ever to be married."

"Oh, you never mean a fiddlestick's end!" said Priscilla, as she arranged her discarded dress, and closed her bandbox. "Who shall *I* have to work for when Father's gone, if you are to go and take notions in your head and be an old maid, because some folks are no better than they should be? I haven't a bit o' patience with you—sitting on an addled egg forever, as if there was never a fresh un in the world, One old maid's enough out o' two sisters; and I shall do credit to a single life, for God A'mighty meant me for it. Come, we can go down now. I'm as ready as a mawkin *can* be—there's nothing a-wanting to frighten the crows, now I've got my ear droppers in."

The point is that the Misses Lammeter are, in Raveloe terms, fine ladies; but they speak like everyone else. Raveloe's is a surprisingly homogeneous society, with no wide range of rank or wealth.

There is Squire Cass:

He was only one among several landed parishioners, but he alone was honoured with the title of Squire; for though Mr. Osgood's family was also understood to be of timeless origin—the Raveloe imagination having never ventured back to that fearful blank when there were no Osgoods—still, he merely owned the farm he occupied; whereas Squire Cass had a tenant or two, who complained of the game to him quite as if he had been a lord.

The gentry of Raveloe are scarcely less naïve than the rustics, their lives almost as confined and sequestered.

It is, however, in the character of Dolly Winthrop that the folk-wisdom of Raveloe is fully realised as the truth of feeling. Dolly is that rarest character in fiction, a positively good person. She is not in the least sentimentalised but shown in her daily actions of charity, carried out almost at the unconscious level, since the doing of them is, as it were, a natural thing. Here, she is a totally successful character as Dinah Morris, for instance, is not.

We see her with Marner on the Sunday morning before Christmas:

"Dear heart!" said Dolly, pausing before she spoke again. "But what a pity it is you should work of a Sunday, and not clean yourself—if you *didn't* go to church; for if you'd a roasting bit, it might be as you couldn't leave it, being a lone man. But there's the bakehus, if you could make up your mind to spend a twopence on the oven now and then—not every week, in course—I shouldn't like to do that myself—you might carry your bit o' dinner there, for it's nothing but right to have a bit o' summat hot of a Sunday, and not to make it as you can't know your dinner from Saturday. But now, upo' Christmas day, this blessed Christmas as is ever coming, if you was to take your dinner to the bakehus, and go to church, and see the holly and the yew, and hear the anthim, and then take the sacramen', you'd be a deal the better, and you'd know which end you stood on, and you could put your trust in Them as knows better nor we do, seeing you'd ha' done what it lies on us all to do."

George Eliot tells us that Dolly made her exhortation "in the soothing, persuasive tone with which she would have tried to prevail on a sick man to take his medicine, or a basin of gruel for which he had no appetite."

As one reads *Silas Marner*, one feels of George Eliot (as one sometimes does of Hardy) that only a radical free-thinker cut off from her (or his) roots could have had quite so intense a nostalgia for the traditional past.

But besides the delineation of country life and humour and of a world gone for ever, there is something else in *Silas Marner*—the moral vision which is, in a sense, the spine of the story. It is a myth of rebirth, but it is also a novel of re-demption. It has a double action, Marner's and the young Squire Godfrey Cass's. Marner is the unwitting agent of Cass's redemption, just as Cass's behaviour is the unwitting cause of Marner's rebirth. But, as George Eliot observed to Blackwood, "The Nemesis is a very mild one," for all that the novel contains one of her most intransigent statements of her moral view: "Favourable chance . . . is the god of all men who follow their own devices instead of obeying a law they believe in. . . . The evil principle deprecated in that religion is the orderly sequence by which the seed brings forth a crop after its kind." In *Silas Marner*, certainly, the seed brings forth the crop after its kind. Retribution falls on the guilty: Cass is punished for his youthful sin through his daughter Eppie's refusing to acknowledge him as her father and cleaving to Marner. Yet, of the two facets of the novel, that of rebirth and that of redemption, it is the first that is dominant, and thereby the novel obtains much of its power to move and to delight, for the myth of rebirth takes us beyond morality.

Chance in *Silas Marner*

Donald Hawes

In this essay, Donald Hawes discusses Eliot's use of chance as a dramatic tool to further the events in her novel. In her fictional world, unexpected or accidental development seem to favor those who believe in providence and duty. Those, like Godfrey, who tend to rely on chance to further their lives never benefit from the unexpected. One may read this as a sign of Eliot's reproval of selfish characters, but Hawes suggests that the inconsistent application of chance throughout the novel may be due to Eliot's divergence from her original conception of the book as a "legendary tale" to one with more realistic overtones. Donald Hawes has done research on Victorian authors. He has edited Thackeray's *Pendennis*, the Everyman edition of Dickens's *Barnaby Rudge*, and the Who's Who series edition of *Who's Who in Dickens*.

George Henry Lewes, encouraging Marian Evans to write fiction, said that she had 'wit, description, and philosophy', which he thought went 'a good way towards the production of a novel', but at the same time he distrusted her 'possession of any dramatic power'. . . . 'Wit, description, and philosophy' had been marked characteristics of Marian Evans's essays and reviews and also, one assumes, of her conversation. By saying 'dramatic power', Lewes, the experienced drama critic, may have had the theatre in mind, since the phrase suggests the ability not only to write striking and memorable dialogue and action but also to create personages and events that convey, in their interrelationship, the significance of the novel. In other words, Lewes seems to be stating that Marian Evans had the capacity to think profoundly about human behaviour and to express herself effectively but that she possibly lacked the novelist's essential technique to embody thought and emotion in fictional charac-

Excerpted from "Chance in *Silas Marner*," by Donald Hawes, *English*, 1982. Reprinted with permission from The English Association.

ters. This distrust, it hardly needs saying, proved generally unjustified, but I think there is at least one example in George Eliot's fiction where her 'dramatic power', though clearly evident, falls short in its generation and support of the 'philosophy' associated with it. 'Dramatic power', the prerequisite of the novelist, and 'wit, description, and philosophy', desirable qualities of the writer of prose of thought, are not blended to make a fully satisfying work of fiction.

ELIOT'S IDEAS ON CHANCE AND DUTY

In *Silas Marner,* George Eliot's sternest passage of moralising comes at the end of Chapter 9, when she comments on Godfrey Cass's habit 'of hoping for some unforeseen turn of fortune, some favourable chance which would save him from unpleasant consequences'. She fancies that 'favourable Chance . . . is the god of all men who follow their own devices instead of obeying a law they believe in', and she proceeds to enumerate instances of irresponsible and reprehensible conduct, the results of which can be mitigated only by Chance, according to the beliefs of their perpetrators. 'The evil principle deprecated in that religion', she concludes, 'is the orderly sequence by which the seed brings forth a crop after its kind'. In expressing her trust in the justice and inevitability of cause and effect, she was, of course, expressing a commonplace of mid-nineteenth-century thought, manifesting itself in studies, for example, of education, history, psychology, and biology. . . . In her review of Robert William Mackay's *Progress of Intellect* (1850), Marian Evans wrote that 'it is this invariability of sequence which can alone give value to experience and render education in the true sense possible'. Detached from the novel, George Eliot's 'sententious prosing about the worship of chance', to use the unkind phrase of an anonymous reviewer of *Silas Marner* is obviously unexceptionable and typical in that it accurately expresses the belief in logical sequence held by her and many of her contemporaries. It is a passage of 'philosophy' that would be completely at home in one of her essays.

But her advocacy of obedience to 'a law they believe in' leaves 'law' undefined. Remembering her opinions expressed elsewhere, we can guess that this is not so much a rational law of causation as a code of conduct which is necessarily associated with such a law, involving diligence, altruism, and self-discipline—in short, Duty, as expressed in her famous pronouncement to F.W.H. Myers in the Fellows' Garden of Trinity College, Cambridge, 'on an evening of rainy May', when she asserted 'how peremptory and absolute' Duty was. 'Never, perhaps', Myers commented, 'have sterner accents affirmed the sovereignty of impersonal and unrecompensing Law'. Although Duty may be for her the primary law, her use of the indefinite article in her statement in Chapter 9 of *Silas Marner* seems to indicate that she would be satisfied simply with any law, believing that adherence to a set of moral rules, no matter what, is worthier and more desirable than independent, unsanctioned actions and ideas. Now her depiction of the Lantern Yard sect in *Silas Marner* shows a valid law in operation, unquestioningly accepted by all the religious community. The principles of their church were so clearly defined as to exclude the prosecution of a criminal and to justify the drawing of lots to discover the thief who took the bag of church money. The sect therefore believed in Chance as well as a 'law'. George Eliot's 'dramatic' presentation shows us that adherence to a law can be reconciled with a trust in Chance, and that the two are not mutually exclusive, despite the implication of her opening remarks in the passage of 'philosophy' in Chapter 9. The questions raised in Silas's mind (and in ours) by the results of the drawing of lots are not explored, or rather—to put it bluntly—are evaded. At the end of the novel, the complete disappearance of Lantern Yard, perhaps justifiable for vaguely symbolic reasons, frustrates Silas's search for an explanation.

THE INFLUENCE OF CHANCE ON SILAS AND GODFREY

Leaving aside that instance as a relatively minor inconsistency, we find more awkward discrepancies between her philosophising and her portrayals of Silas and Godfrey. As a result of the workings of Chance, as revealed in the drawing of lots in Lantern Yard, Silas comes eventually to lead his deadened existence in Raveloe, with no belief remaining in any law except that of the urge to acquire gold. He attains his redemption through a series of events brought about by Chance: Dunstan's theft of his gold, the route taken by Mollie, and his cataleptic fit at the time when the golden-haired Eppie toddles into his cottage. All these happenings, over which he has no control, combine to restore him to humanity and to allow time for love and social and family relationships to develop. Chance is solely responsible and leads him to a law in which he can fully believe, instead of replacing such a law, thus virtually reversing George Eliot's dictum.

But it is Godfrey who is the object of her disapproval in the passage under consideration. And with him she is even more contradictory, since she shows that his reliance on Chance was completely beneficial. Thanks to the disappearance of Dunstan, the death of his first wife, and Silas's adoption of Eppie, he is saved from having to make shameful revelations, particularly to his father and Nancy. His marriage to Nancy, approved in Raveloe as an appropriate match, is reasonably happy, despite their childlessness and her prejudice against adoption, since it is based on mutual tolerance and affection. The discovery of Dunstan's skeleton, after a comfortably long interval, precipitates his avowal of parenthood and his rejected offer to adopt Eppie, and these actions in turn confirm his wife's sympathetic understanding of him

---

QUOTATION ABOUT PROVIDENCE FROM *SILAS MARNER*

A belief in providence dictated many characters' actions. In the following excerpt from the novel, Nancy describes her trust in providence and her disbelief in those who would attempt to act in spite of it.

It was one of those rigid principles, and no petty egoistic feeling, which had been the ground of Nancy's difficult resistance to her husband's wish. To adopt a child, because children of your own had been denied you, was to try and choose your lot in spite of Providence: the adopted child, she was convinced, would never turn out well, and would be a curse to those who had wilfully and rebelliously sought what it was clear that, for some high reason, they were better without. When you saw a thing was not meant to be, said Nancy, it was a bounden duty to leave off so much as wishing for it. And so far, perhaps, the wisest of men could scarcely make more than a verbal improvement in her principle. But the conditions under which she held it apparent that a thing was not meant to be, depended on a more peculiar mode of thinking. She would have given up making a purchase at a particular place if, on three successive times, rain, or some other cause of Heaven's sending, had formed an obstacle; and she would have anticipated a broken limb or other heavy misfortune to any one who persisted in spite of such indications.

George Eliot, *Silas Marner: The Weaver of Raveloe*. Harmondsworth: Penguin, 1972, pp. 216–17.

and bring about his redemption by means of his recognition that his retribution is a just one. Owing to Chance, he is a sadder and a wiser man, who has been fortunate enough to avoid causing a full measure of suffering to himself and others. An adherence to a law of Duty, such as George Eliot advocates in the passage at the end of Chapter 9, might well have led to injuries and anger—to a hurt and indignant Squire Cass, a heart-broken Nancy, perhaps a warped Eppie, a shamed and embittered Godfrey, and, above all, to a completely purposeless and unenlightened Silas Marner. As Leslie Stephen tartly observed: 'His meanness answers admirably. . . . He is freed from all fear of exposure, marries the right young woman, and has, on the whole, a successful life. This may console people who think that the justice of Providence is called into play too clearly'.

The operations of Chance, benefiting both Silas and Godfrey, take place amongst people with an unquestioning belief in Providence. Dolly Winthrop trusts in the tender-heartedness of 'Them above' (ch. 16), and Nancy thinks it wrong 'to try and choose your lot in spite of Providence' (ch. 17). Silas is putting into words a fundamental idea held by the rural community when he agrees with Dolly: 'there's dealings with us—there's dealings' (ch. 16). It therefore seems inconsistent and even unjust that George Eliot should reprove Godfrey for relying upon Chance whilst Silas escapes her censure. An apparent reason for this difference between authorial attitudes is that Godfrey consciously depends on Chance whereas Silas is unwittingly helped by it. There may also be traces of class-feeling in her criticism of Godfrey. Her villagers are not unduly romanticised. In fact, it is usually accepted that they are realistically and convincingly portrayed, in accordance with her explicit repudiation of 'cockney sentimentality' in the treatment of rustic life. Nevertheless, they are seen as possessors of near-Wordsworthian virtues, whereas Godfrey has a weakness of character that derives from the indulgence of his father, who 'had kept all his sons at home in idleness' (ch. 3). And, to make matters worse, Godfrey is insensitive to the feelings of the poor. It 'had never occurred to him that Silas would rather part with his life than with Eppie' (ch. 17), although with a charitable understanding as typical as her moral sternness George Eliot points out that 'he had not had the opportunity, even if he had had the power, of entering intimately into all that was exceptional in the weaver's experience' (ch. 17).

ELIOT'S INCONSISTENCY CONCERNING CHANCE

A more telling reason for her inconsistency concerning people's trusting in Chance may lie in her departure from her initial conception of the novel. 'It came to me first of all, quite suddenly, as a sort of legendary tale, suggested by my recollection of having once, in early childhood, seen a linen-weaver with a bag on his back; but as my mind dwelt on the subject, I became inclined to a more realistic treatment', she wrote to [her publisher] John Blackwood. Nevertheless, as she also told Blackwood, she had 'felt all through as if the story would have lent itself best to metrical rather than prose fiction, especially in all that relates to the psychology of Silas, except that, under that treatment, there could not be an equal play of humour'. Bearing in mind the fact that 'the weight of the clear central contrast falls rather on accident than on character', we can perhaps agree that her first, sudden conception and her prevalent feeling while writing the novel were right after all. A 'metrical' version of 'a sort of legendary tale', incorporating the chief concerns of the novel as well as Silas's psychology, might have more accurately realised the theme of redemption, in that it might have been more disciplined and more schematically patterned than the prose version she actually wrote. I know that George Eliot was not a markedly successful poet. But prose allowed her, like all Victorian novelists, to be discursive, and accordingly to fill in the outline, as it were, with the kind of description, dialogue and comment for which readers have always been deeply thankful—as well as with the 'play of humour' which she thought necessary. The passage on Chance proves that 'wit, description, and philosophy' were at her command, as Lewes knew. At the same time, scene after scene in *Silas Marner* demonstrates the 'dramatic power' which Lewes feared she might lack. Unfortunately, the flexibility of prose as a medium also seems to have given her the latitude to respond spontaneously and over-freely as the narrative prompted, and one result of this licence was her ready generalisation at the end of Chapter 9. The further, wider result was the discrepancy between her 'philosophy, and her 'dramatic' presentation of character and event. So I would suggest that a formalised, 'legendary' treatment, instead of a rendering of 'legendary' material in the 'realistic' mode she chose to adopt, might have helped to align and reconcile all the qualities Lewes mentioned. The movements towards redemption experienced by both Silas and Godfrey might have then been realised in such a way that the moral issues would be not only embodied in people and action but also expressed in authorial comment consistent with the 'dramatic' elements. Marian Evans, the possessor of 'wit, description, and philosophy', would have been completely replaced by George Eliot, the possessor of 'dramatic power' as well as the three former qualities. The consequence might not have been the provision of answers to the questions posed by the claims of Duty and the temptations of Chance but at least the reader might not have been disturbed by the discordances that exist in the novel George Eliot has given us.

Natural Human Relations and Their Influences

David Carroll

David Carroll's article examines Eliot's worldview as reflected in *Silas Marner*. Carroll discusses the concept of a prisoner in solitary confinement and relates that experience to Silas Marner's life before Eppie's appearance. Carroll then traces Silas's and Godfrey's metamorphoses through their relationships with others, but most importantly with Eppie. Carroll believes that Silas's metamorphosis reflects what Eliot termed the "truth of feeling," which could only be reached through the influences of pure and natural human relations. David Carroll has written extensively on George Eliot. Some of his books are *George Eliot and the Conflict of Interpretations, A Reading of Novels* and *George Eliot (The Collected Critical Heritage: 19th Century Novelists)*. Carroll has also edited editions of *Silas Marner* and *Middlemarch*. This article is excerpted from his Introduction to *Silas Marner* in a recent edition for Penguin Press.

Silas Marner explores the origins of folk myth in a rural community at the beginning of the nineteenth century. As a natural historian of religion, George Eliot is seeking to refine her ideas in a world she is most familiar with and where myth-making can be seen at its most primitive. There are several features of life in Raveloe that bring out this anthropological side of the novel. First, the community is remote in time and space, providing the narrator—and the Victorian amateur folklorist—with vestiges and remnants of a distant past to be deciphered: 'Such strange lingering echoes of the old demon-worship might perhaps even now be caught by the diligent listener among the grey-haired

Excerpted from the Introduction, by David Carroll, to *Silas Marner*, by George Eliot. Introduction and Notes copyright ©1996 by David Carroll. Reprinted with permission from Penguin Books, UK.

peasantry.' And beyond these echoes, there are vestiges of an even more remote, mythical past to which the novel reaches out: 'In the early ages of the world, we know, it was believed that each territory was inhabited and ruled by its own divinities.' Though superseded, such myths are an integral part of the genetic, evolutionary history through which we come to understand ourselves. 'The gods of the hearth exist for us still; and let all new faith be tolerant of that fetishism, lest it bruise its own roots.'

Secondly, the novel creates a world full of mysterious gaps and uncertainties. Beyond Raveloe is an inexplicable region from which strangers manifest themselves like apparitions, or into which people disappear without explanation. Some things come (a child), others go (the gold). A dominant image is that of a lighted candle or lantern surrounded by encroaching darkness. Within the community, too, there are social gaps between the landed parishioners and their tenants that are accepted as unbridgeable and eternal, 'the Raveloe imagination having never ventured back to that fearful blank when there were no Osgoods.' And this particular mystery is sharpened by a new development in George Eliot's fiction, the double plot of Silas and Godfrey Cass, which reflects these social divisions and in which the interconnections are minimal and mysterious. A further gap is the narrative hiatus of sixteen years between the two parts of the novel, whose significance becomes fully apparent only in the climactic debate.

To underline the indeterminacies of this fictional world even further, George Eliot endows the central character with catalepsy, 'the chasm in his consciousness,' which baffles both the brethren of Lantern Yard and the rustics. This is an essential feature of the novelist's experiment in the basic logic of myth-making. . . . The challenge of the novel is to depict a world unaccountable at many levels so that the crucial strategies by which people make sense of their lives may be explored in the most fundamental way. This is what separates the major characters, Silas and Godfrey, from the community. Whereas Raveloe relies on its shared beliefs, that mixture of superstition and religion which finds expression in its public rituals—the Sunday church service, the New Year's dance, the discussions in the Rainbow—the protagonists experience a series of sudden dislocations that make them revise repeatedly their ways of looking at life. To both of them can be applied the phrase that describes Silas's career: his 'inward life had been a history and a metamorphosis.' The history belongs to the developing cause and effect of fictional narrative; the metamorphosis to legendary story. *Silas Marner* combines them so that they illuminate each other.

SILAS IN "SOLITARY CONFINEMENT"

These are some of the features which enable the novelist to carry out her most fundamental experiment into what constitutes a minimally coherent myth or world-view. And the narrative commentary repeatedly refers the reader to even more extreme situations. Silas's desperate weaving, for example, is explained in these terms:

> Have not men, shut up in solitary imprisonment, found an interest in marking the moments by straight strokes of a certain length on the wall, until the growth of the sum of straight strokes, arranged in triangles, has become a mastering purpose? Do we not wile away moments of inanity or fatigued waiting by repeating some trivial movement or sound, until the repetition has bred a want, which is incipient habit?

The prisoner in solitary imprisonment, Silas Marner, the author and the reader, are all brought together in the inescapable need to create meaning and purpose in a vacuum. And one of the best places to examine the relationship between the need and its expression is in those primitive communities untouched—unlike the Victorian reader—by critical self-consciousness. 'To people accustomed to reason about the forms in which their religious feeling has incorporated itself, it is difficult to enter into that simple, untaught state of mind in which the form and the feeling have never been severed by an act of reflection.' The novelist enters this untaught state of mind, and then, through the disrupted careers of the protagonists, separates form and feeling, before finally reuniting them in order to examine and redefine their relationship.

The parallel careers of Silas and Godfrey, out of which the novel is constructed, dramatize the creation of mythical systems in response to the unpredictable. The retrospect of the first chapter shows how the religious sect of Lantern Yard has developed its own system of belief, a form of Calvinistic Dissent, in response to 'the currents of industrial energy and Puritan earnestness' of a northern city. Its vulnerability is revealed by the disputes over the meaning of

Silas's cataleptic fits, and then by the theft of the church money. The trusting community which believes that immediate divine intervention, rather than an examination of the evidence, will answer their questions, has produced its darker progeny in William Dane, Silas's rival, who cunningly exploits the situation for his own purposes. When the drawing of the lots declares Silas guilty, he blasphemes against 'a God of lies, that bears witness against the innocent,' and leaves Lantern Yard as Dane's plotting becomes clear to him. In the search for absolute assurance, things have become their opposites: the certainty of divine intervention finds expression in the randomness of the lots, and innocent trust has generated devilish cunning.

The exile into which Silas moves is a limbo 'in which the past becomes dreamy because its symbols have all vanished, and the present too is dreamy because it is linked with no memories.' This blank must—and it is one of George Eliot's imperatives—be filled with some minimal coherence if Silas is to remain a recognizable character. He has to be reconstructed virtually *ex nihilo*, from nothing. All he carries with him into exile is his skill in weaving, but around this a miniature creation myth is enacted as he weaves himself back into existence. The stages are carefully defined. First, with both past and future cancelled, the threads of his weaving criss-cross the emptiness of his life. 'He seemed to weave, like the spider, from pure impulse, without reflection.' And the commentary provides the gloss for the educated reader: 'Every man's work, pursued steadily, tends in this way to become an end in itself, and so to bridge over the loveless chasms of his life.' Then, Silas begins to find in the gold he earns a purpose in life: 'that habit of looking towards the money and grasping it with a sense of fulfilled effort made a loam that was deep enough for the seeds of desire.' A new world is emerging in which time now acquires a structure and meaning: 'the money had come to mark off his weaving into periods, and the money not only grew, but it remained with him.' Silas's 'life [is] narrowing and hardening itself more and more into a mere pulsation of desire and satisfaction that had no relation to any other being', and yet, past, present and future are being linked meaningfully together. Then, as the gold pieces begin to provide continuity in his life, Silas comes to love them as 'his familiars' and enjoy their companionship. And, finally, he celebrates his new life by creating a ritual, his Midas-like 'revelry', which expresses this vivid fetishism. At night he locks the door and closes his shutters, bringing out the golden guineas—the sacraments of his belief—for his love and worship. 'He spread them out in heaps and bathed his hands in them . . . and thought fondly of the guineas that were only half earned by the work in his loom, as if they had been unborn children.' It is a wonderfully vivid account of a world of meaning conjured into existence by the mechanical and minimal rhythm of Silas's weaving.

SILAS'S METAMORPHOSIS

Through this account of Silas's early life and his fifteen-year exile, Eliot is establishing the basic pattern of the novel, the metamorphosis of one world-view into its opposite. In this case, absolute trust in the divine has been replaced by materialism, the miraculous by the mechanistic, simple trust by self-dependence, and the believing community by a life of solitary utility. In neither case, George Eliot implies, is Silas fully human. His original naïve defencelessness, with his 'deer-like gaze', disengaged him from the world, while his embittered reaction has simply turned him into the engine that drives his loom. Having lost his god, Silas has turned himself into a machine for making gold. Though the phases of his life are not completely exclusive—the narrator is at pains to remind us that his 'sap of affection was not all gone'—these are the extreme polarities that have to be reconciled. And it is at this point that the Cass family, from the other mysterious half of the novel, intervenes in his life through the theft of his gold. Again, a 'sudden chasm' has opened up in his life but now he can only '[fill] up the blank with grief.' How can he begin to make sense once more out of his dereliction? Was it a thief or a supernatural power 'which had delighted in making him a second time desolate?' This is the question that Silas, in his helplessness, is now forced to carry into the community.

He finds no clear answers. Instead, we have George Eliot's parody of the contemporary Victorian debates in theology and history as to the nature of evidence and its interpretation. But he has, crucially, been brought into the community, where he is initiated by his Job's 'comforters' into a new way of looking at his affliction. It is a mystery that Dolly Winthrop benignly explains through 'her simple Raveloe theology', which combines 'trust i' Them as knows better nor we do' with good works, those two dimensions of life fatally separated in the first two stages of Silas's career. He has learnt that help must come from outside, and this is why on New Year's Eve he is waiting expectantly with his door open when he is again arrested 'by the invisible wand of catalepsy.' The second impingement of the Cass family upon Silas's life then occurs with the arrival of the child and, with it, the most sudden metamorphosis in the novel. As his gold is transubstantiated into Eppie's curls before his eyes, Silas begins to evolve his third mythical explanation.

The event itself is neither good nor evil. It is how he responds to it; and, as with Job, the question is, what has survived his afflictions? The sudden discovery recalls to Silas the key events of his previous life, but these are now transformed by his response to Eppie, his act of intuitive love, a revelation to himself. It is upon this act of faith and natural affection that he begins to articulate the new myth of his life: 'My money's gone, I don't know where—and this is come from I don't know where. I know nothing—I'm partly mazed.' Encouraged by Dolly to trust in this mysterious rhythm of life, Silas tentatively expresses the hidden logic of events: 'Thought and feeling were so confused within him, that if he had tried to give them utterance, he could only have said that the child was come instead of the gold—that the gold had turned into the child.' This is the minimal confession of faith out of which the legend is finally constructed. And just as the mechanical repetition of the weaving generated one creation myth, so this mysterious sequence generates another, a contrary one, which links him organically to the community from which he has been isolated. Eppie 'created fresh and fresh links' between Silas and Raveloe: 'As the child's mind was growing into knowledge, his mind was growing into memory: as her life unfolded, his soul, long stupefied in a cold narrow prison, was unfolding too, and trembling gradually into full consciousness.' Through Eppie, 'he had himself come to appropriate the forms of custom and belief which were the mould of Raveloe life.' It is through love's mediation that Silas begins to gain possession of his life along with that of the community.

GODFREY'S METAMORPHOSIS

In the other half of the novel, the career of Godfrey Cass undergoes its own metamorphoses which chart the origins, self-contradictions and establishment of his coherent vision of the world. The context here, in contrast, is the aimless, indulgent and bored life of the rural landowners whose repetitive rituals are, in a compelling phrase, their only means of 'annulling vacancy.' With the deft economy she employed in Lantern Yard, George Eliot again delineates in the Cass family a genealogy of world-views. The power in this semi-feudal society is Squire Cass, a widower, who is, unpredictably, both harsh and indulgent. His two sons have responded in contrasting ways, becoming, like Silas and Dane, polar opposites dangerously separated. Godfrey's passive creed is a belief in 'some unforeseen turn of fortune, some favourable chance which would save him from unpleasant consequences,' while the decisive Dunstan believes actively in his own good luck, which he pursues with 'diabolical cunning.' This is why Godfrey has to use him as his agent and intermediary. And through this agency, Dunstan expresses his brother's shadowy and illicit desires—his wish to marry the desirable Nancy, his 'good angel', with its accompanying dark corollary, his wish for the death of the 'demonic' Molly. Their interdependence is expressed vividly in their mutual recriminations, their reciprocal threats to tell all to the squire, and their shifting of responsibility on to each other. In this way, by means of a legend-like genealogy, George Eliot dismantles the indulgent tyranny of the father into the mutually hostile world-views of the sons, a passive reliance on chance and a cunning self-interest. Separated from each other, faith and works are again shown to be corrupting and self-defeating.

From this perspective, those mysterious interventions in Silas's life become successive expressions of the Casses' world-view—the loss of gold becomes theft, the arrival of Eppie becomes her abandonment by her parents. For Godfrey, initially, it is as if his belief in the god of 'favourable Chance' has paid off: Dunstan, the blackmailer, has disappeared; the clandestine wife, Molly, is dead; and their unacknowledged child will now be looked after by Silas. But, in George Eliot's fiction, 'the orderly sequence by which the seed brings forth a crop after its kind' never falters; and it is always initiated by the response characters make to events. In this crisis, Godfrey first hopes that his wife is dead, and then fails to claim his own child:

> The wide-open blue eyes looked up at Godfrey's without any
> uneasiness or sign of recognition: the child could make no
> visible [or] audible claim on its father; and the father felt a

> strange mixture of feelings, a conflict of regret and joy . . .
> when the blue eyes turned away from him slowly, and fixed
> themselves on the weaver's queer face.

It is a momentous pause in which nothing apparently happens, but it is the turning-point of the novel. What Godfrey
mistakenly thinks is the 'deliverance from his long bondage'
is, in reality, Silas's—and Godfrey's own—punishment.

Godfrey's marriage to Nancy is both his salvation and his
nemesis. The Lammeter family, as the other main landowners in Raveloe, represent contrasting values to the Casses, as
their surnames suggest. The head of the family is a sober,
strong-minded widower, with two contrasting daughters. After the sixteen-year gap in the novel, we see that Nancy's
sense of propriety, conventionalism and exactitude have
transformed Godfrey's view of the world. Chance has given
way to routine, order and accountability. But amid this order
there is one omission, variously described as a 'blank' or a
'void', which corresponds to the gap in the text for the
reader. This is their childlessness, which both unites and
separates them. Godfrey seeks to repair the omission
through the adoption of Eppie, but Nancy denies him this
compensation for within the rigidly ordered Lammeter
world there is a strong belief in providence, the acceptance
of the *status quo*, the opposite of the chance from which she
has rescued Godfrey.

EPPIE AND SILAS'S LOVE

Their married years run parallel to Silas's fostering of Eppie
in the time-gap (sanctioned by legend) between the two
parts of the novel. This hiatus represents both steady growth
and sudden metamorphosis in the two main characters
when we rejoin the narrative. This occurs with the discovery of Dunstan's body. Godfrey's growing sense of order and
retribution now turns into a full confession and acceptance
of all omniscient divine power: 'Everything comes to light,
Nancy, sooner or later. When God Almighty wills it, our secrets are found out.' Her shock is followed by Godfrey's
when she replies: 'Do you think I'd have refused to take [Ep-
pie] in, if I'd known she was yours?' This finely prepared
mutual misjudgement is an essential part of what the novelist called the mild nemesis of the story. But now, having reversed his earlier belief in chance, Godfrey is ready to accept
his full responsibility in a divinely ordered universe, as he

and Nancy set off to claim their daughter.

To whom does Eppie belong? In the weaver's cottage, the 'contest', as it is called, takes place between the two fathers with the recovered gold on the table. Who will get which? What principle will settle this semi-legal contest of a paternity suit? The reader has been well prepared for the difficulties attending the assessment of evidence upon which truth-claims can be based. The divided structure of the novel has guaranteed that all the major events are ambivalent— someone's loss is another's gain—while, in addition, the precise interpretation of these events is determined by particular world-views. Silas has passed from the other-worldliness of Lantern Yard through the machine-like world of his weaving to their synthesis of his life with Eppie. Now that the gold has been found, he is at his moment of 'transfiguration,' in possession of his whole life and its meaning. Godfrey, on the other hand, is now intent on claiming Eppie as the 'blessing' denied his marriage and so putting to rights his sixteen years of secrecy and irresponsibility, impatient of any obstacles to 'his virtuous resolves.'

Against Godfrey's claims of legality, duty and blood, Silas invokes . . . the claims of lived experience: '[T]hen, sir, why didn't you say so sixteen year ago, and claim her before I'd come to love her . . . ?' And later, 'Your coming now and saying "I'm her father" doesn't alter the feelings inside us. It's me she's been calling her father ever since she could say the word.' Godfrey wants, in the terms of the novel, the 'form' without the 'feeling'. But the proof is in the naming and the feelings that justify it, just as Silas's naming of Eppie had established their covenant in the first place. This is the basis of Silas's claim. And he is now in a position to justify it by an interpretation of events which finally exorcizes his earlier blasphemy. He combines the language of Lantern Yard with that of Raveloe: 'God gave her to me because you turned your back upon her, and He looks upon her as mine: you've no right to her! When a man turns a blessing from his door, it falls to them as take it in.' What was before a simple sequence—gold, child—now becomes a more complex statement of cause, effect and purpose, a kind of theology. Silas's 'transfiguration' at this moment is the final metamorphosis that encapsulates his whole career, his becoming fully human.

The final decision, the verdict in the trial, however, is left to Eppie, the living evidence of that sixteen-year time-gap in the novel, and the confirmation of one man's blessing and the other's nemesis. The princess in exile chooses to stay with her foster-father by reaffirming, in suitably biblical rhythms, the covenant Silas had made in adopting her. 'And he's took care of me and loved me from the first, and I'll cleave to him as long as he lives, and nobody shall ever come between him and me.' The domestic reality out of which this statement comes is vividly dramatized, as Silas and Eppie, always conscious of each other, touch and hold hands in their cottage. It is a complex and moving scene, which recuperates the whole of the double narrative: two views of the world, painfully evolved, confronting each other. And, as so often in George Eliot's novels, there is no key of interpretation, no general principle, but only an appeal and confession. The appeal is to the sixteen-year gap in the novel during which Eppie has become the incarnate history of Silas's love. With great simplicity she confesses this as the evidence which ensures the keeping of their covenant.

ELIOT AND THE "TRUTH OF FEELING"

Though the life and values of 'the poor who are born poor' are unintelligible to Godfrey and Nancy, they accept Eppie's decision and Silas's judgement, and through this rejection Godfrey is forced, in turn, to move on. He now begins to reconcile the passive reliance on chance of his earlier life with its opposite, his belief in a strictly providential order, neither of which has brought him his daughter. He, too, comes to acknowledge the evidence of the sixteen-year gap in the narrative, the final chasm to be bridged. This sad acceptance is expressed in terms of organic growth: 'While I've been putting off and putting off, the trees have been growing—it's too late now.' This is the darker side of the community's belief in earned good luck. Neither he nor Silas is allowed to go back into the past, pay off their debts, clear up the mystery, and start afresh—for even Lantern Yard has disappeared when the weaver returns there at the end of the novel. It is left to the community, gathering in front of the Rainbow for Eppie's wedding, to authorize the interpretation of events that will pass into legend, that 'strange history' of Silas Marner by which 'he had brought a blessing on himself by acting like a father to a lone motherless child': 'and all differences among the company were merged in a general agreement with Mr. Snell's sentiment, that when a man had deserved his good luck, it was the part of his neighbours to wish him joy.'

If *Silas Marner* is a novel about a legend and its creation, what truth does the legend embody? A clue is to be found in a letter George Eliot wrote to her evangelical friend Sara Hennell on 9 October 1843, shortly after losing her Christian faith, where she recapitulates the stages of her own developing beliefs. First comes the liberation 'from the wretched giant's bed of dogmas', then the enjoyment of 'the full use of our limbs and the bracing air of independence', but soon the sense of 'our own miserable weakness' introduces a new awareness: 'Speculative truth begins to appear but a shadow of individual minds, agreement between intellects seems unattainable, and we turn to the *truth of feeling* as the only universal bond of union.' For George Eliot, the individual life develops, as we have seen, by a series of disruptive discoveries and disconfirmations. But finally . . . all the partial truths fall away to reveal the genuine kernel of belief, the truth of feeling.

This truth of feeling has, however, to find expression in a recognizable form. To express his new-found sense of community and love, Silas Marner appropriates 'the forms of custom and belief which were the mould of Raveloe life'. But he could do this only after the forms and feeling of his previous beliefs had been dismantled; and the same applies to Godfrey Cass. In a similar way, the novelist appropriates and refashions traditional beliefs of various kinds in her narrative and commentary. . . . All are assimilated finally to express, in her words, 'the remedial influences of pure, natural human relations'. This, in brief, is George Eliot's mythical method. Out of a conflict of personal myths emerges one generally accepted by the community, a myth that develops from these and genetically contains them. Silas's 'strange history' confirms the Raveloe belief in earned good luck, a belief that encapsulates, without resolving, the agency of chance and that of cause-and-effect, out of which this novel—like all novels—is so strikingly constituted.

CHAPTER 3

Characters and Their Motivations

READINGS ON SILAS MARNER

Characterization in *Silas Marner*

Joan Bennett

In this article, Joan Bennett explores the development of individual characters in *Silas Marner*. Bennett discusses the need to suspend disbelief about some of the improbable events in the early part of the story, but stresses how once that disbelief is suspended, the individual characters in the novel are completely consistent and believable. Bennett concentrates on diverse characters such as Dolly Winthrop and Nancy Lammeter and her sister Priscilla, emphasizing their sharply delineated characterization, which Eliot develops through the characters' own words and actions—not through patronizing commentary. Joan Bennett has written extensively on literature, including two books on the author Virginia Woolf. This article is excerpted from the book, *George Eliot: Her Mind and Her Art*.

The first period of George Eliot's creative activity ends with *Silas Marner*, conceived and completed between the end of November 1860 and March 1861. The story of *The Weaver of Raveloe* is a poetic conception and it was in this light that George Eliot herself thought of her story of a man, simple and trusting by nature, who, by the deliberate act of a false friend, is accused and convicted of theft. He is sundered from the community in which he was rooted and deprived at one blow of his faith in man and God—for his guilt had been 'proved' by the simple method of drawing lots and he and his co-religionists believed that the divine hand would point out the sinner. Isolated from his kind, he goes to live among strangers, and gives his heart to the lonely accumulation of gold. Then he is drawn back into the health-giving life of the community by a child. In February 1861 George

Excerpted from *George Eliot: Her Mind and Her Art*, by Joan Bennett. Copyright ©1962 by Cambridge University Press. Reprinted with permission from Cambridge University Press.

111

Eliot wrote to [her publisher] Blackwood, who had been reading the first chapters:

> I don't wonder at your finding my story, as far as you have read it, rather sombre: indeed, I should not have believed that any one would have been interested in it but myself (since Wordsworth is dead) if Mr Lewes had not been strongly arrested by it. But I hope you will not find it at all a sad story, as a whole, since it sets—or is intended to set—in a strong light the remedial influences of pure, natural human relations. The Nemesis is a very mild one. I have felt all through as if the story would have lent itself best to metrical rather than to prose fiction, especially in all that relates to the psychology of Silas; except that, under that treatment, there could not be an equal play of humour. It came to me first of all quite suddenly, as a sort of legendary tale, suggested by my recollection of having once, in early childhood, seen a linen weaver with a bag on his back; but as my mind dwelt on the subject, I became inclined to a more realistic treatment.

It is fortunate that George Eliot decided to write her story in prose. She was incomparably more gifted as a prose than as a verse writer; her blank verse works of fiction are conscientious, competent and dull. In them the preconceived moral idea is always obtrusive because, when she composes in verse, she is never swept onward by the flow of creative energy. Moreover, as is evident in what she here writes to Blackwood, she shared the widespread mid-nineteenth-century view that 'metrical composition' implied a peculiar solemnity.

According to her own account, if she had written the book in verse, she would have felt bound to exclude the 'play of humour', which is an important factor in its success. Another is the freshness and apparently effortless freedom of its style which is partly due to her confidence in the story as adequate to convey its own moral, so that didactic asides hardly occur, and partly to the spontaneity and speed of composition which would almost certainly have been slowed down if she had chosen verse as her medium.

SUSPENDING DISBELIEF

Nothing was lost by writing in prose provided the reader has no inhibiting preconceptions about the nature of prose narrative. He must be ready to accept improbable events as readily as he would accept them in a poem, for the story is undoubtedly improbable. But once the framework of the plot is accepted the truth to life, within that framework, is convincing. We must willingly suspend disbelief when we discover that the first Mrs Godfrey Cass, having poisoned herself with drugs, has died at a convenient spot, after walking some miles through the snow, carrying a child old enough to toddle. She must have been unusually strong, for a child of that size is not easy to carry; but that is to consider too closely. We must believe—and the author beguiles us into belief if we will allow her—that the golden-haired baby leaves the dead mother at a point just near enough to Silas's cottage for it to totter into it and so be found, a living substitute for the lost golden hoard. Further, we must accept the coincidence that Dunsey Cass falls into the stone pit near-by, and that his corpse and Silas's stolen treasure are not discovered until sixteen years later, on the eve of Eppie's marriage. Nor must we question the likelihood that Nancy's baby daughter died in infancy and that Nancy and Godfrey could never have another child. None of these things is in itself impossible. The reliance on coincidence to bring about the redemption of Silas and the 'mild' Nemesis for Godfrey is much less than the reliance [author Thomas] Hardy often puts on it to translate his more pessimistic vision. Once these events are accepted the conduct of the story carries conviction; Silas, Eppie and Godfrey behave with entire consistency and develop in accordance with their nature.

CREATING CHARACTERS

George Eliot's fertility of invention and assurance in the creation of character is the more remarkable in *Silas Marner*, since her choice of the place and time for her story excludes any character whose intellectual and moral experience resembles her own. . . . But, in Raveloc, 'in the days when the spinning-wheels hummed busily in the farmhouses', no one suffers from intellectual hunger. George Eliot has here escaped from her own world of intellectual curiosity, as well as from the life of the city, which she was finding oppressive. On 28 November 1860, she wrote in her journal:

> Since I last wrote in this Journal, I have suffered much from physical weakness, accompanied with mental depression. The loss of the country has seemed very bitter to me, and my want of health and strength has prevented me from working much—still worse, has made me despair of ever working well again. . . . I am engaged now in writing a story—the idea of which came to me after our arrival in this house, and which has thrust itself between me and the other book I was meditating.

Her rustic tale served her, among other things, as a means of rediscovering the rural world for which she was homesick and in which she could focus her attention on the Wordsworthian 'primary pains and pleasures' of simple people.

The community of Raveloe is confined, spiritually and intellectually, within the narrow bounds of early nineteenth-century village life. The Christian observances, baptism, Sabbath-keeping and occasional communion are accepted within the community as semi-magical rites or as pious customs.

> The inhabitants of Raveloe were not severely regular in their churchgoing, and perhaps there was hardly a person in the parish who would not have held that to go to church every Sunday in the calendar would have shown a greedy desire to stand well with Heaven, and get an undue advantage over their neighbours—a wish to be better than the 'common run' that would have implied a reflection on those who had had godfathers and godmothers as well as themselves, and had an equal right to the burying-service.

There is so little curiosity about the fundamental Christian doctrines (as distinct from Christian ethics and Christian customs) that Dolly Winthrop cannot discover anything in common between her religion and the Methodism in which Silas had been brought up. When, after the loss of his money, she goes to try and comfort him she suggests that he would be happier if he went to church with his neighbours at any rate

> . . . 'upo' Christmas-day, this blessed Christmas as is ever coming',

and Silas answers:

> 'Nay, nay, I know nothing o' church. I've never been to church.'

> 'No!' said Dolly, in a low tone of wonderment. Then bethinking herself of Silas's advent from an unknown country, she said, 'Could it ha' been as they'd no church where you was born?'

> 'Oh yes', said Silas, meditatively, sitting in his usual posture of leaning on his knees, and supporting his head. 'There was churches—a many—it was a big town. But I knew nothing of 'em—I went to chapel.'

> Dolly was much puzzled at this new word, but she was rather afraid of inquiring further, lest 'chapel' might mean some haunt of wickedness. After a little thought she said—

> 'Well, Master Marner, it's niver too late to turn over a new leaf, and if you've niver had no church, there's no telling the

good it'll do you. For I feel so set up and comfortable as niver was when I've been and heard the prayers, and the singing to the praise and glory o' God, as Mr Macey gives out; and Mr Crackenthorp saying good words, and more partic'lar on Sacramen' Day. And if a bit o' trouble comes, I feel as I can put up wi' it, for I've looked for help i' the right quarter, and gev myself up to Them as we must all give ourselves up to at the last; and if we'n done our part, it isn't to be believed as Them as are above us 'ull be worse nor we are, and come short o' Their'n.'

Poor Dolly's exposition of her simple Raveloe theology fell rather unmeaningly on Silas's ears, for there was no word in it that could rouse a memory of what he had known as religion, and his comprehension was quite baffled by the plural pronoun, which was no heresy of Dolly's, but only her way of avoiding a presumptuous familiarity.

DEFINING CHARACTERS

The squirearchy of Raveloe are hardly more sophisticated than the rustics; their mental world is almost as remote from that of their author. But they belong to a realm of thought and feeling that surrounded her as a child and from which her most untrammelled creative power springs. The peculiar quality of the whole book arises from the limitations of the field which excludes all the metaphysical problems with which her mind had been long occupied. The characters, with the exception of the two evil-doers Dunsey Cass and the first Mrs Godfrey Cass—who, when they have set the plot in motion disappear—are all drawn with an easy assurance and persuasive truth to life. They speak in an idiom which is characteristic of a class and a time, but which also sharply defines the individual character. This is as evident with a minor character, such as Priscilla Lammeter as it is with her sister Nancy:

'It drives me past patience', said Priscilla, impetuously, 'that way o' the men—always wanting and wanting, and never easy with what they've got. They can't sit comfortable in their chairs when they've neither ache nor pain, but either they must stick a pipe in their mouths, to make 'em better than well, or else they must be swallowing something strong, though they're forced to make haste before the next meal comes in. But joyful be it spoken, our father was never that sort o' man. And if it had pleased God to make you ugly like me, so as the men wouldn't ha' run after you, we might have kept to our own family, and had nothing to do with folks as have got uneasy blood in their veins.

The tactless, forthright speech is as idiosyncratic as is Nancy's reply in swift defence of her husband.

George Eliot's insight into Nancy's character is unfaltering and never more so than when she allows her to behave in a way that neither the reader nor Nancy's own husband can foresee, when Eppie's real parentage is first revealed to her. Nancy's instinctive moral certitudes and her narrowness of judgement are counterbalanced by a warmth of heart and quickness of sympathy and the two aspects of her nature combine at this juncture to produce the response Godfrey least expects. She had resisted his plea to adopt Eppie when she did not know that Eppie was his child, because adoption conflicted with one of her 'rigid principles'.

> To adopt a child because children of your own had been denied you was to try and choose your lot in spite of Providence. . . .

Her code, made up of custom and of precept, comprised absolutes to govern even small points of manners; before her marriage

> she insisted on dressing like Priscilla, because 'it was right for sisters to dress alike', and because 'she would do what was right if she wore a gown dyed with cheese-colouring'.

When the long-concealed past evil-doing comes to light, no wonder Godfrey expects this rigid naïve moralist to be unforgiving. Yet when she speaks there is no doubt that we hear the authentic accent of her character.

> 'Nancy', said Godfrey, slowly, 'when I married you, I hid something from you—something I ought to have told you. That woman Marner found dead in the snow—Eppie's mother— that wretched woman—was my wife: Eppie is my child.'

> He paused, dreading the effect of his confession. But Nancy sat quite still, only that her eyes dropped and ceased to meet his. She was pale and quiet as a meditative statue, clasping her hands on her lap.

> 'You'll never think the same of me again', said Godfrey, after a little while, with some tremor in his voice.

> She was silent.

> 'I oughtn't to have left the child unowned: I oughtn't to have kept it from you, But I couldn't bear to give you up, Nancy. I was led away into marrying her—I suffered for it.'

> Still Nancy was silent, looking down; and he almost expected that she would presently get up and say she would go to her father's. How could she have any mercy for faults that must seem so black to her, with her simple severe notions?

But at last she lifted up her eyes to his again and spoke. There was no indignation in her voice—only deep regret.

'Godfrey, if you had but told me this six years ago, we could have done some of our duty by the child. Do you think I'd have refused to take her in, if I'd known she was yours?'

Within the neatly articulated, simple, legendary plot of *Silas Marner* George Eliot creates a little world of sharply individualized characters. She presents them mainly by their own words and acts and her own commentary on their behaviour is never over-elaborate and never patronizing. She identifies herself with them and measures the compass of their ideas as securely as though she, herself, had never read any other book than the human heart. The furthest stretch of philosophical speculation in Raveloe is represented by the meditations of Mr Macey, tailor and parish clerk, with which he puzzles and entertains the company at the 'Rainbow' when they prompt him to tell again an old and favourite story about the wedding of the first Mr Lammeter:

'. . . Mr Drumlow—poor old gentleman, I was fond on him—but when he come to put the questions, he put 'em by the rule o' contrary, like, and he says, "Wilt thou have this man to thy wedded wife?" says he; and then he says, "Wilt thou have this woman to thy wedded husband?" says he. But the partic'larest thing of all is, as nobody took any notice on it but me, and they answered straight off "Yes", like as if it had been me saying "Amen" i' the right place, without listening to what went before.'

'But *you* knew what was going on well enough. . . . You were live enough, eh?' said the butcher.

'Lor' bless you!' said Mr Macey, pausing, and smiling in pity at the impotence of his hearer's imagination—'why, I was all of a tremble: it was as if I'd been a coat pulled by the two tails, like; for I couldn't stop the parson, I couldn't take upon me to do that; and yet I said to myself, I says, "Suppose they shouldn't be fast married, 'cause the words are contrary?" and my head went working like a mill, for I was allays uncommon for turning things over and seeing all round 'em; and I says to myself, "Is't the meanin' or the words as makes folks fast i' wedlock?" For the parson meant right, and the bride and bridegroom meant right. But then, when I come to think on it, meanin' goes but a little way i' most things, for you may mean to stick things together, and your glue may be bad, and then where are you? And so I says to mysen, "It isn't the meanin', it's the glue." And I was worreted as if I'd got three bells to pull at once, when we went into the vestry, and they begun to sign their names. But where's the use o' talking—you can't think what goes on in a 'cute man's inside.'

This little novel . . . is the most flawless of George Eliot's works. It is not the greatest since its small scale, its narrow world and its symbolical character precluded the exercise of some of her gifts. But nowhere else does her fiction carry all that she has to say so unobtrusively and effortlessly. It is natural that she should have thought of Wordsworth as the ideal audience for the story of the weaver whose soul withers away to a mere lust for gold when he is shut off from his kind by despair and then flowers again to full humanity when events draw him back within the community. And perhaps this is the only one of her books that was written throughout in the Wordsworthian mood of 'wise passiveness', and springs without conscious intellectual effort from 'emotion recollected in tranquillity'.

The Joys of Fatherhood

Caroline Arthurs

In this selection, Caroline Arthurs discusses Eppie's influence on Silas. She indicates that Eppie helps awaken certain traits that were dormant in Silas's nature. Arthurs also explores Silas's role as a father (how his character decides what type of father he will be) and Nancy and Godfrey's roles as potential parents. Arthurs ends by discussing Eliot's views on parenthood and her recognition that parenting requires active care and dedication.

'A child, more than all other gifts
That earth can offer to declining man,
Brings hope with it and forward-looking thoughts.'

George Eliot takes these lines from Wordsworth's 'Michael' as part of the title-page for *Silas Marner*. Although the idea contained in the lines is a commonplace, it is characteristic of Eliot to scrutinize ordinary beliefs and behaviour with an intelligence that exposes the moral complexities operating within the commonplace. *Silas Marner* is an extensive exploration of the meanings of Wordsworth's words, as a story about the hopes—and responsibilities—that a child offers to one 'declining man'.

APPROACHES TO *SILAS MARNER*

There is a popular idea that *Silas Marner* is a kind of fairy-tale and is different from Eliot's other novels because its narrative is patterned by chance, fate and co-incidence rather than by individual choice and action. . . . 'The key-word is Dolly's "trusten": "All as we've got to do is to trusten, Master Marner—to do the right thing as fur as we know, and to trusten. For if us as knows so little can see a bit o' good and rights, we may be sure as there's a good and a rights bigger nor what we can know."' I suggest that although Dolly Winthrop's acceptance of Providence convinces Silas, it does

Excerpted from "*Silas Marner:* The Uncertain Joys of Fatherhood," by Caroline Arthurs, *English,* 1988. Reprinted with permission from The English Association.

not square with a full reading of the text. In fact, the author, who is not Dolly, implies doubt about providential power and justice, suggesting rather that individual thought and action contribute largely to human happiness. In her exploration of fatherhood, which is the *raison d'etre* of *Silas Marner*, Eliot demonstrates that decisions, commitments, hesitancies, relationships are matters of individual moral choice. Individual choice determines the pattern of events in the book's main area of concern—that is the relationship of adult with child.

Elements of fairy-tale, co-incidence, and fate do influence the mood and tone of the book and several specific events are matters of chance. By chance, Molly, Eppie's mother, dies at a point most timely for Godfrey and for the subsequent development of the plot. By chance, one of Silas' fits coincides with Eppie's toddling past him towards the light of the cottage. And the beginnings of the story are long ago and far away, reflecting its original inspiration. Eliot records that the idea for Silas Marner sprang directly from her childhood. 'It came to me first of all quite suddenly, as a sort of legendary tale, suggested by recollections of having once, in early childhood, seen a linen weaver with a bag on his back . . .'. But while a 'legendary' tale implies a representative, symbolic, generalised quality, in fact Eliot 'became inclined to a more realistic treatment' and *Silas Marner* is specific and particular in all its aspects. Perhaps Eliot moved away from a legendary conception at the same early stage of writing when she abandoned the metrical form in favour of prose. But she does adhere to the child-like quality of her original idea and her finished novel maintains throughout that immediate, uncomplicated clarity of vision which characterizes memories from childhood.

EPPIE'S INFLUENCE ON SILAS

We are familiar with the novelist who writes about the adult world from the child's point of view: . . . *Silas Marner* is particularly interesting and unusual because it explores, conversely, the impact of a child on the adults around her. Therefore it raises questions about the nature of parenthood; questions which are Eliot's response to Wordsworth's lines.

The early part of *Silas Marner* shows Silas as a 'declining man' not just in the broad Wordsworthian sense of his ageing, but more specifically because he loses his faith, his community, his 'forward-looking thoughts' through the treachery of William at Lantern Yard. Gradually, after Eppie's dramatic entry into Silas' life, that decline is reversed. Because Silas becomes a parent, because of the kind of parent he is, because of his circumstances, Silas is able to unlock the doors which separated him from his past, his emotions, his community, and hope. Silas believes that by her presence in his life, Eppie has automatically conferred these blessings on him. That is the simple direct link he makes between her and the happiness he achieves. However, Eliot shows us that the kinds of fulfillment associated with Eppie are neither necessary nor automatic but are achieved by the conscious and unconscious behaviour of all those, like Dolly and Godfrey, who take some responsibility for the child.

Some innate, though long dormant, aspects of Silas' own personality determine the kind of father he becomes. Before being banished from Lantern Yard he had felt and expressed affection. He had loved Sarah, and his friend William; and had also the deep-buried memory of a baby sister, whom he had carried in his arms, who died, and whose memory he chooses to revive by naming Eppie after her. Silas' timid tender-heartedness, stunned by William's treachery and its consequences, stirs again only when the child toddles into his house, the first person Silas encounters in Raveloe who needs protection and help which he can give. The affectionate desire to protect and help is part of Silas' nature; it impels him towards Eppie and informs all his upbringing of the child. And that sense of duty, which has secured Silas respect and a degree of acceptance in Raveloe, means that when he formally undertakes responsibility for Eppie it is a wholehearted, patient commitment.

Unquestioning commitment and loving protectiveness are essential bases of the success of Silas' relationship with Eppie and they are dormant in his nature before Eppie comes and he allows her to awaken them. Although Silas' response to her does come from the depths of his nature, it is also within his control. He allows himself to respond. Godfrey Cass, also capable of love and compassion, moved by the child's beauty, knowing that she is his own, yet chooses not to form a bond with her. Eliot is careful to show that whatever our sentimental beliefs may be about children's interests and wisdom, in fact the adults make the choices, however slight or half-thought-out or impulsive those decisions are. As the child grows, Silas, sensitively, changes with her. He's willing to suspend his weaving to look with Eppie at flies crawling in the wintry sun. He will abandon the loom altogether to sit in the fields with her. And there he re-admits memories of his mother's wisdom about the mysterious healing powers of plants. These are matters of choice. Silas could decide not to interrupt his work but to satisfy Dolly's eager longing to care for Eppie, as substitute for the daughter she never had. Instead he chooses to respond to Eppie, to keep closely aware of her needs, thoughts and feelings; and this takes up more time as the years go by. Silas' fatherhood is the soil in which Eppie's affection roots, grows and flourishes. It is not a neutral medium. Silas maintains the soil with time, patience and imaginative sensitivity.

Hitherto self-sufficient in Raveloe, Silas begins to recognise that in order to nurture Eppie he needs to take account of surrounding circumstances, to co-operate with the community, whose practical and spiritual wisdom is embodied in Dolly Winthrop. Jealous though he is of Dolly's maternal encroachments, Silas is bound to recognise Eppie's needs and allows Dolly to provide for her clothes and her laundry. Dolly's instinctive tact in encouraging Silas to bathe Eppie is comparable with his own when he is gauging Eppie's feelings; and Dolly is comparably rewarded by maintaining Silas' confidence and gradually becoming a kind of mother to Eppie.

SILAS AS A FATHER

Eliot shows that commitment to bringing up a child is physically and emotionally strenuous and that parents' efforts change but do not lessen with time. *Silas Marner* does not gloss over these unromantic facts. Dolly is still washing Eppie's clothes sixteen years after her arrival in Raveloe. Godfrey has continued unobtrusively to pay for Eppie's care and therefore Silas lives in an enlarged cottage, provides some schooling as well as food and clothes for Eppie, and can keep and feed the animals which give her so much pleasure. Yet Silas' own ability to earn money has declined during the sixteen years, not principally in his case because of the general decline of the weaving trade in that period, but because his time is increasingly taken up by care of the child. The coal-hole episode is a rich example of the kinds of energy Silas expends on Eppie. First Dolly obliges him to consider the new and puzzling matter of disciplining his young child.

He has then to explain Eppie's wrong-doing and punishment to her. The execution of the punishment causes him much fear, doubt and guilt. Eppie and her clothes have all to be cleaned afterwards. And then they all have to be cleaned again because Silas has not been able to frighten the child and she goes back into the coal-hole on purpose. So all Silas' efforts achieve only the realisation that he cannot punish Eppie and cannot therefore take any of the short-cuts by which correction leads to acceptable behaviour. Eppie will need his active care all of her waking hours, except when Dolly takes charge of her.

Silas' character determines what kind of father he is. But circumstances also foster the companionship which develops with Eppie and which Godfrey and Nancy come to envy. For sixteen years Silas is supported by money, advice, time and practical help, without which that relaxed and confident intimacy could not have grown so strong. Eliot seems to be simply endorsing two of the common cliches about children. One is that they bring happiness: the other is that they take care of their parents' old age. Of course Eliot is not re-iterating folk-wisdom. She is exploring it. We have seen that the happiness Silas feels through his adoption of Eppie is achieved partly through continuing, various efforts of his own, partly through the energies of other people, and partly by chance. And his happiness is accompanied by anxiety and vulnerability. Silas is anxious for Eppie's future, as he becomes frailer and less able to provide for her and as his eventual death comes closer. He is vulnerable because all his affections are intense and they all focus on her as they once focused on the life of Lantern Yard. In his youth, those affections were attacked and destroyed and in his maturity his emotions are equally vulnerable because they are concentrated again. This emotional vulnerability is not a necessary part of being a parent but does accompany the intensities of pleasure which Silas feels through Eppie. Wordsworth knew this too. 'Michael' is also the tale of a man passionately bound to his child. When Michael's son is exiled, his own hopes are destroyed. In Wordsworth's story, a parent's emotional dependence becomes the reason for his sorrow.

But not in Silas' case. Chance, or the shaping imagination of the novelist, provides an ideal partner for Eppie. Aaron, who is strong, handsome, familiar, morally correct, in love with Eppie, represents one of the fairy-tale or providential aspects of the story. The presence of Aaron within the novel conveniently secures for the reader the conventional happy ending of marriage. But Eliot allows us to see that from Silas' point of view this satisfactory securing of the future has been an uncertain business. Eppie will be provided for, she will not leave him, there will be no guilt for him to feel: but these possibilities were all real and could have been fulfilled. Eliot is aware of them and their presence is felt behind the arrangements which she chooses to make for ending her story.

NANCY AND GODFREY AS POTENTIAL PARENTS

Silas Marner's apparent security in his companionship with Eppie has been enviable to Godfrey Cass and, in a less direct and personal way, to Nancy. Nancy is deeply conventional and had accepted the conventional wisdom that children complete a marriage, that marriage is not fulfilled without them. But after the sorrow of her baby's death Nancy gradually becomes reconciled to what she understands as an act of fate, or chance, or the will of God, that there will be no children for her and Godfrey. She understands with such conviction that she can oppose Godfrey's urging her to adopt a child. To adopt Eppie means, for Nancy, a deliberate flouting of nature and God's will, a futile defiance which is inevitably self-destructive. If she and Godfrey adopt a child, things will turn out badly, she believes. Marriage and motherhood were her hopes; but if her hopes are thwarted she has the strength to accept that and the resilience to turn her hopes and energies elsewhere. The image of Nancy sitting alone in a quiet house on a Sunday afternoon, failing to divert her thoughts with a worthy book, is a melancholy one. But Nancy feels no self-pity.

The flaw in Nancy's serenity is Godfrey's self-pity. Having chosen to deny Eppie, he cannot or will not accept the results of his choice. He watches his child grow and thrive, partly because of his own gifts of money, and he envies Silas' obvious happiness. Godfrey's regret is natural in an impulsive, warm-hearted person and we would think him cold if he did not covet some of Eppie's daughterly affection. But we have also seen that child-rearing is difficult and that its rewards are not inevitable. Godfrey was unable to face even the initial difficulties inherent in claiming rights over Eppie: the shame, secrecy and disgrace of his first marriage made an insuperable obstacle for him. On the other hand, the difficulties for Silas of taking responsibility for Eppie did not seem insuperable to him. For each man, the strength of the difficulties is actually a matter of perception, of subjective judgement, weighed against the desire to love and protect.

Sixteen years on from Eppie's arrival in Raveloe, Godfrey is discontented, his envy of Marner is festering. We begin to see Godfrey as characteristically dissatisfied: if he had adopted Eppie, for example, would he then have longed for a son too, to inherit his name? Nancy accepts their childlessness and would let their lives move forward, not checked by regret, but for her husband's inability to accept his lot, the lot that he, unlike Nancy, had consciously chosen. It is difficult, then, to sympathise with Godfrey. Here is a different sort of example of Eliot's realistic unsentimentality about parenthood. Far from endorsing Godfrey's belief that children, or just Eppie, would make him happy, she indicates that he is likely to be always discontented, that he has no conception or imagination of the pains that accompany the pleasures of bringing up a child, and that regret may take the form of destructive self-indulgence. 'Dissatisfaction, seated musingly on a childless hearth, thinks with envy of the father whose return is greeted by young voices—seated at the meal where the little heads rise one above another like nursery plants it sees a black care hovering behind every one of them, and thinks the impulses by which men abandon freedom, and seek for ties, are surely nothing but a brief madness.' So Godfrey is not being punished by Dolly's 'Providence' for disowning his child, but indulging himself in regret. Although Nancy looks for other sources of 'forward-looking thoughts,' Godfrey chooses not to.

ELIOT'S PERCEPTIONS OF PARENTHOOD

Eliot shows that 'the clear perception that life never *can* be thoroughly joyous' may be a matter of choice. We see this not only in Nancy, but in her sister, Priscilla, who protests too much for our conviction that she prefers to be an old maid. We see it in Dolly's moralisings about the place of human suffering within her scheme of religious conviction. We see it in Silas' acceptance that the truth about the theft at Lantern Yard will never be known. Sometimes the past must be let go and some hopes abandoned. Dolly justifies her wisdom in terms of faith and trust in Providence. Eliot, more sceptical about divine justice, suggests that such acceptance is wise because it enables life to go forward.

If this is conventional agnostic wisdom, then much of what Eliot has to say about our moral experience and behaviour does amount to that. Her power is in exploring the reasons and circumstances and implications that support her wisdom, in the imagination that makes her truths vivid. In *Silas Marner* she explores adult perceptions and experiences of parenthood and because the story is coloured by the sense of the fairy-tale, of rural idyll, its conclusion is suitably affirmative and celebratory. It is appropriate that Silas' fatherhood is conventionally rewarded with a loving, beautiful daughter whose future is provided for and who will provide for him, both materially and emotionally. At the same time Eliot is clear sighted about the years of active care that have necessarily preceded the reward and how precariously it has been achieved.

The serenity at the close of *Silas Marner* is far removed from the sombre conclusion of 'Michael', in which hope and forward-looking thoughts have been destroyed. In *Silas Marner* the hopes of a 'declining man' are fulfilled in Eppie's marriage to Aaron. Eliot has sustained the positive mood of the lines which she chose from 'Michael' as her text and has brought her theme to a different conclusion from Wordsworth's. Although chance and circumstance play their part in her tale, its conclusion is neither forced nor capricious but above all the outcome of choice.

The Significance of Nancy Lammeter Cass

Terence Dawson

Terence Dawson examines the importance of a seemingly minor character, Nancy Lammeter Cass, in relationship to the novel's plot and George Eliot's own life. Dawson explores Nancy's role with regard to several other characters, including Silas, Godfrey, and her own father. Moreover, he draws parallels between the isolation that Silas experiences and the isolation that Nancy experiences. Ultimately, Dawson argues that Nancy's story is pivotal to the development of important themes in the novel. Terence Dawson is a Senior Lecturer at the University of Singapore. He is the coeditor of the book, *The Cambridge Companion to Jung.*

Silas Marner (1861), always a favourite with readers, was until recently considered too obvious and too lightweight to merit serious critical discussion. On the surface, the main plot would seem to be about the regeneration of a middle-aged weaver through love and his reintegration into the community in which he lives. Interlinked with this 'story' is another, generally described as the story of Godfrey Cass, the local squire's eldest son, who turns over something of a new leaf in the course of the events described. Faced by a novel in which there are two distinct plots, the critic's first task is to discover the connexion between them. The most frequent definition of the relation between the two stories in *Silas Marner* is that they are parallel, but move in opposite directions. Not only is this view too vague to be helpful, it is also misleading, for there is no similarity whatsoever between Silas's situation at the beginning and Godfrey's at the end, or vice versa. Nevertheless, the two plots are unquestionably related: indeed, I shall argue that they show many

Excerpted from "'Light Enough to Trusten By': Structure and Experience in *Silas Marner*," by Terence Dawson, *Modern Language Review*, 1993. Reprinted with permission from the author.

more similarities than have been identified to date.

In purely narrative terms, the main events of the novel would seem to trace the parallel stories of the weaver and Godfrey Cass: I do not wish to argue otherwise. But in psychological terms, because the novel was written by a woman, one would expect it to reflect and describe a woman's experience. . . . A primary aim of these pages is to argue that embedded in the surface narrative of *Silas Marner* are numerous thematic concerns which suggest that the events it describes are shaped by a psychological dilemma pertinent to Eliot at the time of writing. My intention is to show that the very structures of the text invite the reader to read this novel as an expression of a woman's psychological concerns.

INTRODUCTION OF NANCY

My first objective is to demonstrate that the events of *Silas Marner*, not only those of the main plot but all the major events, including such scenes as the wonderfully comic conversation in the Rainbow Inn, can be shown to be directly related to a female character who functions as the 'carrier' of the author's unconscious personality. This character, I shall show, is Nancy Lammeter, an apparently minor figure hitherto almost completely ignored by critics.

Surely one of the most striking features of this novel is the way in which it shifts from all almost exclusive emphasis on male characters, especially in the first nine chapters, to all emphasis on female characters, especially in the much shorter Part 2. It is worth comparing what each of the main characters achieves between the outset of the events and their conclusion. The theme of a novel can often be discovered by comparing the situations with which it opens and closes. *Silas Marner* begins in late November or early December of about 1803, with a description of Silas as a recluse and a miser, and it ends in May or early June of about 1819, with an account of Eppie's marriage to Aaron. The most obvious transformation effected is Silas's integration into the community, but he is not, as [critic] Joseph Wiesenfarth maintains, the only character to change significantly in the course of the novel. There are three other principal characters, Eppie, Godfrey, and Nancy, whose situations are also radically altered between these dates. At the outset, Eppie is an infant whose mother, Molly Cass (née Farren) is not in a condition to take proper care of her, and the novel ends with an account of Eppie's marriage. But she is an infant during the major scenes, and even in Part 2 she is never truly individuated, and for these reasons it would be difficult to relate the other events (such as the Lantern Yard episode or the scene in the Rainbow) directly to her change of circumstances. Godfrey and Nancy both undergo a significant change. At the outset, the engagement which they both had hoped for has all but fallen through; at the end, they reaffirm their love for one another. Because there is more emphasis on Godfrey in the early chapters, critics have been tempted to ask how the weaver's story relates to his. Nancy, however, plays a much more emphatic role in Part 2 than does her husband. Although she is no less directly transformed by the events than Silas, Eppie, and Godfrey, her function in the novel has never been adequately explained.

Nancy's role in Part 1 is not immediately evident. She is first mentioned in Chapter 3, where the narrator describes the villagers' collective supposition that 'if Mr Godfrey didn't turn over a new leaf, he might say "Good-bye" to Miss Nancy Lammeter'. A few moments later it is revealed that Godfrey is already married. In other words, Nancy has not only been jilted, she is being cheated. It is not, however, until Chapter 11, almost halfway through the text, that she makes her first appearance at Squire Cass's New Year party, but from this moment her importance increases. Part 1 closes with a reference to her marriage with Godfrey, and at the beginning of Part 2, the narrator all but tells the reader to pay special attention to her. This is how she is reintroduced:

> Perhaps the pretty woman, not much younger than [Godfrey], who is leaning on his arm, is more changed than her husband [. . .] to all those who love human faces best for what they tell of human experience, Nancy's beauty has a heightened interest [. . .]. The firm yet placid mouth, the clear veracious glance of the brown eyes, speak now of a nature that has been tested and has kept its highest qualities.

Given this signalling, it is astonishing how few critics have found anything substantial to say about her. She is central to every chapter in Part 2. Even Eppie's wedding, with which the novel ends, coincides with Nancy and Godfrey consolidating their own marriage. In the following pages I shall argue that the events in which Godfrey is involved should be read not as his, but as *Nancy*'s 'story', by which I mean that, in spite of her being a less prominent character, the events that make up this part of the novel can all be shown to be directly related to *her* concerns.

The basis for this claim is derived from the analysis of the major episodes of the novel, all of which reveal thematic parallels with the dilemma of confronting Nancy. Even when she does not actually feature in the episodes in question, or plays only a minor role in them, the insistence with which their theme is related to her amounts to evidence that the entire narrative constitutes a symbolic representation of the dilemma facing her. My aim, then, is to demonstrate that not only is the so-called sub-plot principally about a process affecting Nancy, but so too is the entire novel: in other words, to reveal that the interconnected plots of the novel tell *one* story on two distinct 'levels' of fictional representation and to argue that, in psychological terms, both pertain to Nancy. In the first section, I look at the parallels between the two 'plots' to show that the events in which Godfrey features can indeed be said to be told from Nancy's perspective. In the next, I identify the nature of the dilemma confronting her. . . . I then examine the relation between the Silas plot and the way in which Nancy achieves a tentative resolution to this problem and, lastly, as my reading tacitly implies that the experience at issue was highly relevant to the author, I briefly relate the conclusions to George Eliot's situation in 1860–61.

SIMILARITIES BETWEEN SILAS AND NANCY

First, let us remind ourselves of the main stages of Silas's story. At the outset of the novel, he is living in complete isolation, nursing the hurt of a wrong done to him some fifteen years previously by William Dane and the arbitrary result of the drawing of lots by the Lantern Yard brethren. On the day of Mrs Osgood's birthday party, his gold is stolen. A month later, he sees lying on his hearth a baby girl, the sight of which awakens 'old quiverings of tenderness' in him. Sixteen years later, contrary to his fear that she might abandon him, Eppie chooses to stay with him, and the novel ends with her marrying Aaron. This pattern is remarkably similar to that of Nancy's story. At the time the novel opens, Nancy is privately nursing the hurt of a wrong done her by Godfrey. On the night of Mrs Osgood's birthday party, Dunstan falls to his death in the stone-pits, and some four weeks later, Molly dies while on her way to claim recognition, thus making it possible for Nancy to marry the man whom she loves. Fifteen years later, Godfrey, afraid that she might want to leave him, reveals his past to her. To his surprise, she forgives him and they consolidate their relationship. These similarities are striking. Each plot begins with a contrast between two men, one of whom is well-intentioned but weak (Silas, Godfrey); the other, more dynamic but morally reprehensible (William Dane, Dunstan). The men are either brothers or the very best of friends (Silas and Dane are called 'David and Jonathan' by the Lantern Yard brethren). In the 'present', Godfrey's only remaining possession is his horse, appropriately called Wildfire. Even this he is prepared to sacrifice rather than admit to his marriage with a barmaid, Molly Farren, because he knows that his father would disinherit him for such a folly. In the 'past', when William Dane falsely accuses Silas, the latter is literally cast out by the community to which he belongs. Both stories are thus instigated by a similar combination of factors. In each case, a more vital, 'daring and cunning' brother is endeavouring to steal the birthright of a better but weaker brother.

There is, however, a very considerable difference between the two situations. Godfrey does not want his 'degrading marriage' with Molly Farren brought to light; he is guilty of deceiving not only his wife but also Nancy, whom he has continued to court. Silas, on the other hand, does *not* commit the crime he is accused of. If there is a parallel between the events in the 'present' and those in the 'past', it is between Silas and Nancy, who are equally blameless.

One notes that Godfrey's conduct is constantly being excused. We are asked to believe that he really is 'a fine openfaced good-natured young man'. The facts do not bear this out: he is secretive and has behaved abominably towards both Molly and Nancy. He deserves to be disgraced. Why, then, should he not be exposed? Who stands to gain by his behaviour's not being revealed? Most obviously, of course, himself. One remembers that Nancy is proud and could not stand knowing that Godfrey has been deceiving her. At the end, he reminds her why he did not tell her about his marriage with Molly Farren: 'With your pride and your father's, you'd have hated having anything to do with me after the talk there'd have been'. He is, of course, making excuses, but he is also probably right. Everything we learn about Nancy in Part 1 would corroborate his assertion. If she reacts differently in Chapter 18, it is because she has 'changed' by the time he reveals his past to her. In other words, it is essential that Nancy does not learn of his affair with Molly until she is ready to assimilate such information. Nancy would like Godfrey to be exonerated from as much censure as possible, for he can be the man that *she* wants him to be only if *his* shoddy behaviour is not a reflection of his own personality but has been provoked by another character. Thus Dunstan's function is ambiguous. At one level of reading, he seeks to inculpate Godfrey, whom he 'traps' into marrying a barmaid of whom he is ashamed because he wants his older brother 'turned out of house and home' by their father. But at another, Dunstan, by his very existence, serves to extenuate Godfrey's guilt, and in this latter capacity, no matter how paradoxical this may seem, Dunstan serves Nancy's interests.

I shall look more closely at the similarities between Dunstan and William Dane in a moment. Meanwhile, it is worth noting those between Molly and Sarah, each of whom is associated with the stronger but morally reprehensible man: Molly becomes involved with Godfrey through Dunstan, and Sarah marries William Dane. The most striking feature that they have in common is their weakness. Sarah slips into marriage with William Dane and is never mentioned again, and Molly is kept away from Raveloe, in a neighbouring village called Batherley, where she slides into laudanum addiction until she finally succumbs to a longing for oblivion. There is a clear parallel with Nancy's situation. When Godfrey fails to propose to her, Nancy determines not to marry him and withdraws to her own home. Molly's isolation corresponds to Nancy's isolation, and Sarah's preference for William Dane corresponds to Nancy's continuing interest in Godfrey after his behaviour has become as hypocritical as that of William Dane. In thematic terms, then, the fifteen years of Silas's self-imposed isolation correspond to the period of about three years of Nancy's bitter doubts.

In corroboration of this, one notes the parallels between the ways in which Silas and Nancy react to the various wrongs done to them. They both ward off despair by devoting themselves to work. When the lots pronounce against him, Silas ceases to trust in a 'God of lies'. To forget his pain, he abandons his home town, settles in as isolated a community as possible, and devotes himself to his work. Weaving, one of the dominant images of the novel, symbolizes the slow growth of a pattern through the patient interconnexion of opposites. Similarly, when Godfrey fails to propose to her, Nancy abandons all hope of marrying him. To forget her pain, she buries herself in domestic duties: her hands 'bore the traces of butter-making, cheese-crushing, and even still coarser work'. Like linen, butter and cheese are the products of patient toil. Thus, at the outset of the events, both Silas and Nancy have been wronged, and have reacted in a similar fashion. They are both leading isolated and restricted lives, immersing themselves in transformative work in order to forget their hurt.

Nancy is equally central to the crucial events which take place on the evening of Mrs Osgood's birthday party and Squire Cass's New Year party. Mrs Osgood is Nancy's aunt: Godfrey's relations play virtually no part in the story. The night of her birthday party, we learn that Godfrey is very pleased to see Nancy. The same evening, Silas's gold, which stands in lieu of a 'purpose' in his life and is the visible symbol of his 'hard isolation', is stolen, causing him for the first time since his self-imposed exile to become aware of a 'lack' in his life. A few moments later, the thief, Dunstan, disappears from view (we subsequently learn that he has fallen to his death). This not only frees Godfrey from the negative influence upon him which Dunstan represents, but thereby opens the way for him to make things up with Nancy. We know that Nancy is still deeply attached to Godfrey: it is surely legitimate to infer that his pleasure in seeing her causes Nancy to become conscious of the distance that has grown between them—that is, of a 'lack' in *her* life. The theft of Silas's gold thus coincides with Nancy's becoming dimly aware of how she too has 'undergone a bewildering separation from a supremely loved object'.

The parallelism between the two plots is even more apparent on the night of Squire Cass's New Year party. In the course of the festivities at the Red House, Bell Winthrop comments to Mr Macey: 'Well, I think Miss Nancy's a-coming round again'. This remark not only tells the reader that Nancy's determination not to marry Godfrey is not as firm as she would like people to believe, but also, at least in the eyes of one villager, lays the blame for the delayed engagement not with Godfrey, but with Nancy. This is so contrary to one's assumptions about the situation that it requires attention. Only Dunstan knows about Godfrey's secret marriage. No one else suspects Godfrey of anything other than coming under Dunstan's influence. Ben's comment tells us that Nancy appears to have resolved to end her self-imposed isolation by responding to Godfrey's devotion. The dance in the Red House coincides with two crucial events, one occurring just outside the weaver's cottage and the other inside. Molly dies of laudanum intoxication and Silas discovers Eppie on the hearth and begins to feel 'old quiverings of tenderness' for the first time in several years, thereby discovering a 'purpose' in life. Nancy's change of heart thus coincides not only with the death of a woman who is an obstacle to her ambition to marry Godfrey but also with the beginning of Silas's redemption through love. Moreover, the phrases used to describe Silas's emotions are equally applicable to Nancy: she also feels 'old quiverings of tenderness' towards Godfrey and thereby discovers a new 'purpose' in *her* life. Thus, just as Nancy's intimation of Godfrey's continuing affection for her, on the night of Mrs Osgood's birthday party, coincides with Silas becoming conscious of a lack, so her 'a-coming round again' in her attitude towards Godfrey, noticed by Ben on New Year's Eve, coincides with the awakening of Silas's love for another human being.

The ending of the novel reveals further parallels. When the stone-pits are drained, Dunstan's body is found and Godfrey confesses to Nancy that Eppie is his daughter. There is no obvious reason why the salving of Godfrey's conscience is either a satisfactory resolution to the events or in any way relevant to the Silas-Eppie-Aaron story. The ending is much more significant if it is seen as the resolution of a conflict that has faced the two female characters. Nancy forgives Godfrey his deception. The thought of leaving him does not enter her head; indeed, the suggestion is that their union is strengthened by the confession. Eppie also forgives her father for his behaviour, even though she cannot consider leaving Silas, the only father whom she has known. Her decision prepares the way for her marriage with Aaron. The ending of both stories thus involves a similar combination of factors: it puts the commitment and loyalty of the two female characters to the test. But the two characters who gain by this situation are Nancy and Silas, for nothing further can now threaten their happiness.

There are, therefore, remarkable parallels between the two plots. Nancy's story moves in the same direction as Silas's. In the first stage, confused by her own commitment to

Godfrey, Nancy has isolated herself and is working tirelessly at her domestic duties; in the second, she responds again to Godfrey's evident (even if questionable) devotion; in the third, when a situation arises which threatens to leave her once again alone, she chooses to stay with him. In the first stage of Silas's story, he is living in isolation, working tirelessly at his weaving; in the second, he feels 'old quiverings of tenderness' for another human being; in the third, when a situation arises which threatens to leave him once again alone, his fears are quickly dispelled by Eppie's decision. That such extraordinary parallels should exist between these two very different plots implies that Nancy is very much more central to the novel than has been recognized. . . .

THE ONE DIFFERENCE

I have looked at some parallels between Silas's story and Nancy's story. There is however one all-important difference. Silas is acted upon. Things happen to him. He is expelled from the Lantern Yard brethren. His money is stolen and he later discovers Eppie on his hearth. He is not abandoned at the end. When he acts (for example, when he decides to leave the Lantern Yard community, or to look after Eppie) it is compulsively. Silas is never an agent. In contrast, each of the main stages in Nancy's story is characterized by a decision which *she* makes. Her isolation corresponds to *her* determination not to marry Godfrey. Her resolve then wavers; she warms to him once again; at exactly the same time (although she knows nothing of this), she is liberated to marry him. At the end, when provided with a reason which, earlier, would have been sufficient for her to abandon him, she chooses to stay with him. The main events in Nancy's story correspond to her various attitudes and decisions. She *is* an agent. In this section, I want to show, by means of an analysis of the relation between Nancy and the other characters, that all the events are directly related to her: the opening situation offers a symbolic representation of a challenge facing her, and the course of events described in the novel reflects how she reacts to it.

NANCY AND GODFREY

The surprising number of attributes that Nancy and Godfrey have in common provides the most striking indication of the nature of their relation one to the other. Priscilla chides

Nancy for 'sitting on an addled egg for ever, as if there was never a fresh un in the world'. Godfrey is defined by his similar vacillation and moral cowardice. His father describes him as a 'shilly-shally fellow' and adds: 'You take after your mother. She never had a will of her own'. Nancy's mother died when she was a small child, and so too did Godfrey's. Although Nancy is reluctant to admit she loves him, she does not want to marry anyone else, and Godfrey constantly puts off declaring that he loves her, while conceding that there is no other woman whom he wants to marry. One way of looking at the characteristics they have in common is to maintain that they are drawn to one another because of their similar backgrounds. Such an explanation is insufficient. The parallels suggest rather that they 'mirror' one another: in other words, that their relationship is conditioned by psychological factors. Because the Nancy-Godfrey plot tells *her* story, one must conclude that Nancy is drawn to Godfrey largely because he 'personifies' or 'mirrors' aspects of her own weakness. This, in turn, implies that Godfrey is not so much an autonomous male character as a type or, more specifically, an 'image of a man' to which she is instinctively drawn. . . .

Read in this way, the elements that compose the initial situation symbolize the impasse in which Nancy finds herself. At the time the novel opens, both Nancy and Godfrey live in houses dominated by a father-figure (The Warrens by Mr Lammeter, The Red House by Squire Cass). Nancy's sister, Priscilla, is entirely contained in her relationship with her father, she is proud that she 'features' his family and spurns all other men:

> 'The pretty-uns do for fly-catchers—they keep the men off us. I've no opinion of men, Miss Gunn—I don't know what you have. And as for fretting and stewing about what *they'll* think of you from morning till night, and making your life uneasy about what they're doing when they're out o' your sight—as I tell Nancy, it's a folly no woman need be guilty of, if she's got a good father and a good home. [. . .] As I say, Mr Have-your-own-way is the best husband, and the only one I'd ever promise to obey'.

This is not the speech of a liberated woman; it is an expression of Priscilla's over-attachment to her father and a corresponding confusion of 'father' and 'home' that prevent her from even contemplating a relation with a male 'other'. Priscilla does not change: at the end of the novel, she is as attached to her father as she was sixteen years before. She thinks of him as unique and is correspondingly scornful of other men: 'But joyful be it spoken, our father was never that sort o' man'. She never distances herself from him.

At the outset, in spite of her continuing love for him, Nancy has turned her back on Godfrey and is living at home with her sister and father: in other words, she has adopted her sister's maxim. This implies that Priscilla personifies an attitude which Nancy has adopted in spite of its being detrimental to her happiness. . . . Nancy would like to marry Godfrey; instead, she is sitting at home pretending she has forgotten him. If Priscilla personifies an aspect of Nancy's character of which she is unaware, then her opinion about men in general tells the reader what Nancy is unconsciously afraid of: Nancy is worried at what Godfrey might be doing when he is out of her sight. Given that Nancy has no inkling of Molly's existence, her fears must represent tendencies in her own character.

The corresponding events in the Silas plot not only corroborate this claim, but also constitute a direct comment on what she is doing. One remembers that it is on becoming engaged to Silas that Sarah's manner towards him 'began to exhibit a strange fluctuation between an effort at an increased manifestation of regard and involuntary signs of shrinking and dislike'. That is, as soon as Sarah becomes engaged to him, she begins to have negative feelings towards him. She is afraid of his epilepsy, and epilepsy may be defined as an 'absence' from oneself. Silas's 'absences' are equivalent to Nancy's feelings of emptiness when Godfrey goes away for 'days and days together'. We are told that everyone in Raveloe thinks they would make 'a handsome couple', but Nancy turns her back on him in much the same way as Sarah abandons Silas. Imagining that Godfrey is unreliable, she retires to her own home, Yet, although she pretends she does not want to marry him, she continues to treasure some dried flowers for his sake. She cannot bring herself to forget him; later, she asserts that there is no other man that she would ever have contemplated marrying. In other words, she has surrendered herself to Godfrey, but only in her imagination. In reality, she is shunning him. *Silas Marner* offers a vivid representation of how and why such opposite tendencies arise. . . .

On the surface, everything pertaining to Nancy is 'of delicate purity and nattiness', but the other elements which compose the initial situation leave room to doubt whether this is the whole picture. They suggest that she is unconsciously projecting her doubts and suspicions onto those around her, and even weaving plots in order to disguise her fear of committing herself to Godfrey. Indeed, so unconscious is she of this tendency that she ascribes it not to any female character (any aspect of her female identity) but to male characters: not only to Godfrey but also to Dunstan and William Dane.

The connexion between Dunstan and William Dane needs little insistence. Dunstan 'traps' Godfrey into a degrading marriage and William Dane has 'woven a plot' in order to have Silas expelled from the Lantern Yard brethren. Just as Godfrey falls easy prey to Dunstan's blackmail because he does not have the courage to stand up to his father, so Silas falls easy prey to William Dane because he does not have the courage to stand up to the arbitrary decision of the Lantern Yard brethren. Indirectly, however, this trait reflects something happening to Nancy. . . . In the same way as Nancy has adopted Priscilla's views, so Godfrey has come under Dunstan's negative influence. Thus, the quarrel between the two brothers can be seen as a conflict between two components of a woman's animus. The question, then, becomes: 'What reason does the text offer to explain why Nancy should imagine men as behaving in this way?'

Surprisingly, the answer is provided by the two scenes which feature groups of men, for they, too, can be shown to be related to Nancy. The Lantern Yard brethren are defined by their manner of arbitrarily judging a man by drawing lots. Although they are called 'brethren', they act towards Silas more like father-figures. . . .

NANCY AND HER FATHER

Astonishingly, although the conversation at the Rainbow has occasioned a great deal of critical interest, no one has ever offered a reason why it should be entirely about Nancy's father. It consists almost exclusively of groundless and tenaciously defended opinions. The butcher, the farrier, Mr Macey, Mr Tookey, and Mr Winthrop all argue fiercely, each convinced that he alone knows what is right, and its most significant feature is that it is *entirely* about Mr Lammeter: first, about his cows, then about his father's arrival in Raveloe, then about his unusual 'Janiwary' marriage, and finally about the previous owner of his home. One need scarcely add that this is not because he is a close friend of any of them: Mr Lammeter lives a retired existence. A literal reading of the events leads to observations about either social life in an isolated community or typically masculine attitudes. But given the tendency I have noted in Nancy, who is 'as constant in her affection towards a baseless opinion as towards an erring lover', we can infer that the villagers constitute yet another aspect of her animus. Thus, both groups of men described in the novel are associated with arbitrary opinionatedness. The Lantern Yard brethren offer all archetypal representation of the consequences of such a tendency. The villagers tell us that it stems from Nancy's father.

The culminating tale in the extraordinary conversation at the Rainbow is about the previous owner of the Warrens, and it provides the only lengthy description we are given of Nancy's home. Nancy is described as 'slightly proud and exacting'. She is interested only in 'the young man of quite the highest consequence in the parish' and dreams of one day becoming '"Madam Cass," the Squire's wife'. Her pride seems to come from her father. Mr Lammeter, like Godfrey, 'always *would* have a good horse'. Appearances matter to them. It is fitting, therefore, that the previous owner of Nancy's home was a jumped-up tailor with an exaggerated concern with appearances. Determined to impress his neighbours at no matter what cost, Mr Cliff (or Cliff, as he is usually called) built and ran an enormous stable. He so bullied his son into acting like a gentleman that the boy died and, mentally unbalanced, he himself died soon after. The Warrens, where Nancy lives, is still haunted by the sound of stamping horses and cracking whips, which the terrified locals call 'Cliff's holiday'. Nancy has a similar determination to have her own way; Priscilla remarks how Nancy behaved as a child: 'If you wanted to go to the field's length, the field's length you'd go; and there was no whipping you, for you looked as prim and innicent as a daisy all the while'. The reference to 'whipping' is perhaps not entirely fortuitous. The tale of Cliff's holiday, with the stamping of horses and the cracking of a whip, symbolizes Nancy's periodic fits of irrational, headstrong determination, a tendency that has emotionally isolated her.

That the Lantern Yard brethren function as father-figures for Silas, and the conversation in the Rainbow is entirely about Mr Lammeter, suggest that Nancy's problem with Godfrey stems from her relation with her father. . . . Not surprisingly, such a tendency usually stems from an exaggerated attachment to her father in her childhood. Thus, Mr Cliff's relationship with his son may be read as a symbolic representation of the psychological effect that Mr Lammeter has had, unwittingly, upon Nancy. The son who dies is 'equivalent' to the Godfrey on whom Nancy has turned her back. Cliff's holiday is a symbolic description of the irrational aggression which can take possession of a woman and its origins in the foibles of a doting father. . . .

The surface narrative and the deeper structures implied by the text thus produce radically different readings of the events. On the surface, it appears that the reason for Nancy's self-imposed isolation is that her fiancé has jilted her, that the Lantern Yard brethren are just a narrow-minded sect, and that the villagers represent the conversation of rustics. A literal reading of the events can lead only to the conclusion that we should not look too closely at the novel's coherence. A psychological analysis of both structures and themes allows one to admire its coherence. It suggests that Godfrey's irregular attentions correspond to Nancy's fears and that the two groups of men described in the novel symbolize the reason for these fears: she is still so attached to her father that she is reluctant to trust any other man. . . .

The situation at the outset of the novel, in which Nancy is living in self-imposed isolation, in a home which is haunted by the sound of stamping horses and cracking whips, thus symbolizes a 'loss' of her true female identity. She has withdrawn into herself to the point of being almost invisible, and Eppie (the other important female character) is suffering from inadequate attention. In a novel written by a woman, their situation is not only significant but also disturbing.

The novel thus springs from the impasse in which Nancy finds herself as a result of an over-attachment to her father. Her anamnesis is easily deduced. She has grown up, like Priscilla, in an isolated home without a mother, with a tendency to overvalue her father and a corresponding tendency to undervalue other men, which has led to a fear of committing herself to another man. Her fear that Godfrey might not be the kind of man her father would be proud of and a related suspicion of what he might be doing when out of her sight signal a fundamental lack of confidence in her own worth. *Silas Marner* opens with a symbolic expression of the terrible emotional isolation into which a woman who is over-attached to her father can be plunged, causing her to become unconsciously reluctant to marry, and to weave fantasies that risk causing her increasing hurt.

THE INTERWOVEN PLOTS

It is time to look again at the way in which the two plots are connected and to examine further the part played by Silas, the weaver of Raveloe, in the events. Existing definitions of the relation between the two plots are unsatisfactory. It has always been assumed that the events concerning Silas form the main plot, and that those concerning Godfrey form the sub-plot. It is also generally held that the Godfrey plot is the more 'realistic' and that the Silas plot is 'fairy-tale-like', 'mythic', or even 'archetypal'. When considered separately, there is nothing surprising about either of these claims; considered together there is. For if one defines the main plot as archetypal and the sub-plot as realistic, then one is, in effect, claiming that the 'realistic' story serves to elucidate the 'archetypal' events. But a woman does not (at least not in the usual sense of the words) live within an 'archetypal' situation, from which she withdraws at night to dream of 'reality'. By definition, archetypal interactions are a symbolic representation of a 'real' dilemma: a woman living in 'reality' might very well dream of archetypal interactions. Thus, the usual definitions attributed to the two plots, in psychological terms, are problematic. For in psychological terms, the main plot is the one which can be shown to give shape to all the other events described, and it is doubtful whether the Silas plot can explain any of the events in what I have redefined as the Nancy plot. Moreover, in psychological terms, the main plot will inevitably be the one whose interactions are the most realistic. Thus, if the Nancy plot is indeed the more realistic, then one would expect the archetypal events to be a symbolic portrayal of its central concern. In this section, paradoxical though it may appear, I want to demonstrate that the more realistic events of the Nancy plot, in psychological terms, may be defined as the main plot and that the archetypal events of the Silas plot are a symbolic representation of the dilemma facing Nancy. Indeed, given the relation between the two plots, I want to propose that it is Nancy's gradually changing attitude that gives shape not only to the events in which she is, both directly and indirectly, involved, but also to the weaver's story.

This is a bold claim and needs some clarification. Such a relation as I am suggesting might exist between the two plots clearly cannot, in *sensu strictu* [in the strictest sense], be ascribed to any character (for example, Nancy): ultimately, any such relation must stem from the nature of the dilemma confronting the author. However, if the thematic content of the events in the archetypal narrative can be shown to correspond at all times and in all important features with the concerns of the more realistic narrative, then one can assert that the more realistic events shape the course of the archetypal events. Because Nancy is the central figure of the realistic events, one can relate the events of the Silas plot to her changing attitude, even if these are, ultimately, but a reflection of the author's unconscious transformation. My first task, then is to demonstrate in what ways the Nancy plot can be said to give shape to the course of Silas's story. At the outset, Silas is a miser. It is generally conceded that one cannot separate his money from Eppie; in other words, if his affection for Eppie represents a positive quality, then the hoarding of his golden guineas represents a misplaced sense of value. The parallel with Nancy's situation is evident. His purposeless counting of his money symbolizes Nancy's equally purposeless sense of satisfaction during her self-imposed isolation.

Such a parallel suggests that Silas also personifies all aspect of a woman's personality. One notes that he is defined solely by feminine attitudes. Weaving is a craft traditionally associated with women, a point made explicit by one of the villagers: 'You're partly as handy as a woman, for weaving comes next to spinning'. His only social dealings are with the women of Raveloe. His rich knowledge of herbs comes from his mother. The instance given that his 'sap of affection was not all gone' is his love of an earthenware pot, an evidently feminine symbol. He becomes not only a father but also a mother to Eppie. Like Nancy, he comes from the North. Silas is described as 'one of those impressible self-doubting natures'. Nancy is similarly impressible (shown by Priscilla's influence) and equally given to self-doubt. The 'unpropitious deity' from which Silas flees is equivalent to the Godfrey whom Nancy shuns. Silas's sense of benumbed pain is identical to Nancy's, and just as Silas does not want to believe in 'a god of lies', neither does she. The 'clinging life' he leads during his period of hard isolation corresponds to her comparable isolation, during which she 'clings' to her domestic duties. These parallels suggest that Silas, paradoxical though it may seem, personifies a significant aspect of Nancy's personality.

When the lots declare Silas guilty, he shows himself willing to carry the burden of his friend's guilt. He tells William Dane '*You* stole the money, and you have woven a plot to lay the sin at my door. But you may prosper for all that'. This parallels Nancy's desire to exonerate Godfrey from the very guilt which she unconsciously attributes to him. This is perhaps the cornerstone of the novel. For although Nancy feels deeply hurt and imagines the worst about Godfrey, she keeps sufficient hold on herself not to spoil all chance of reconciliation by openly accusing him. The mechanism at work here is delicate. On the one hand, I claim that Nancy is projecting guilt onto Godfrey; on the other, I am saying she never accuses him. There is no contradiction here. What one imagines is not under one's conscious control. Nancy is unconscious of the fears that lead to her imagining Godfrey as married to Molly. It is how she reacts to her situation that is important. It would have been easy for her to become vindictive of this animus/man whose irregular attentions she cannot decipher. That Silas seeks no revenge on William Dane suggests that Nancy nurtures no ill-feeling towards Godfrey. Later, we learn that even when he settles in Raveloe, nothing that the villagers say can 'stir Silas's benumbed faith to a sense of pain'. That is, he remains (deliberately?) unconscious of the injury done to him, just as Nancy seems determined to believe the best of Godfrey. Instead of challenging Godfrey (which would probably have led to their permanent separation), she buries herself in cheese-making. Silas's faith in the outcome of his patient toil symbolizes Nancy's unconscious belief that her patient toil will reveal a solution to her problem.

One cannot change the past, Nancy realizes at the end. At the outset of the events, Eppie is a neglected child, symbolizing Nancy's neglect of her own feminine worth. Eppie is Molly's child, and Molly personifies Nancy's unconscious doubts. And the child must be cared for, even if Nancy is not ready to take responsibility for the 'fantasies' she has spun. Just as Mr Lammeter has unwittingly had a detrimental effect on his daughter's emotional development, so Godfrey abandons Eppie. Another father-figure is therefore needed to right the balance. . . . Silas is a potential father-figure willing to carry the burden of responsibility for Nancy's shadow-personality (represented by William Dane's guilt and Molly Farren's child) and nurture Eppie until Nancy is strong enough to resign herself to the 'lot that has been given [her and Godfrey]'. This is the sense of the 'mysterious burden' carried by weavers in 'that far-off time'. At critical moments and in times of emotional stress, we all need an 'other': that is, an archetypal figure in whom to 'trust', who will carry the burden of our suffering until we are strong enough to assume the responsibility for ourselves. Silas fulfils this role. In other words, he belongs to a deeper level of imaginal experience than Nancy: he is an archetypal image of a father willing to care for Eppie until Nancy is ready to accept fully the specific conditions of her lot. As Sandra Gilbert has pointed out, the daughter-father relationship is the key to the novel, but Eppie is not the only daughter-figure. Nancy, who spans the entire novel, is of far greater significance to the overall structuring of narrative events.

NANCY'S MARRIAGE

The two key events occur in the midst of festivities. Dunstan robs Silas while Nancy is dancing with Godfrey at Mrs Osgood's, and Eppie finds her way to the weaver's door while Nancy and Godfrey are dancing at Squire Cass's New Year party. . . . The harmony of the villagers at this event signals that Nancy's tendency to act upon arbitrary opinions is temporarily inoperant. It is often upon the slightest decisions that everything hinges. It is this crucial change of attitude that allows Nancy to accept Godfrey's invitation to dance with him, which symbolizes their imminent union.

Silas's discovery of Eppie on his hearth, and the unexpected birth of his love for an abandoned creature, represent the renewal of Nancy's love for Godfrey. In other words, Eppie personifies an aspect of her nature that Nancy had been denying (or, in psychoanalytic terminology, repressing). Thus, if the rehumanization of Silas corresponds to Nancy's warming again to Godfrey, then Eppie personifies Nancy's burgeoning love. This is why Eppie has and requires no depth of character: she is an archetypal image of a daughter-figure in an older woman's imagination. It is because

Nancy's difficulties stem directly from her over-attachment to her father that Eppie's education is entirely entrusted to a symbolic foster-father. Silas's growing devotion to Eppie signals a process deep in Nancy's unconscious, working towards the correction of her self-doubts.

Had Godfrey acknowledged Eppie at his father's New Year party, Nancy would have withdrawn still further from society and become another Priscilla: competent, no doubt, but never having had the experience of a relationship. In other words, he would have taken Eppie into the Red House, and she would have been left with only the dried leaves that she treasures for his sake, longing to marry him and have his child. The novel traces the 'process' she has to go through before she is ready to overcome her tendency to long for 'what was not given'. Her dilemma determines not only the course of its two separate stories but also the nature of the interconnexions between them. Silas's redemption through love is a symbolic representation of the way in which Nancy gradually overcomes instinctive tendencies in her personality which might have become detrimental to both her aims and her happiness.

Within a year of Nancy's 'a-coming round again', she and Godfrey marry. Her continuing desire to do everything 'well' is represented in the archetypal story by the untiring assistance which Eppie's god-mother lends Silas. Dolly Winthrop personifies all unconscious level-headed matronly devotion to duty that allows Nancy to retain her self-respect throughout both her period of isolation and her childless marriage. Dolly thus functions as a 'positive' aspect of Nancy's shadow. It is wholly appropriate that it should be an aspect of Nancy's feminine personality (a woman's shadow is an image of a woman) that should chide Silas . . . for not having more trust. It is Dolly who tells Silas he must learn to 'trust i' Them as knows better nor we do'. He is partly but not entirely convinced.

Fifteen years after their marriage, Godfrey confesses to Nancy the truth about Eppie. By forgiving him (or, more accurately, by not using his confession as a reason for destroying their present relationship) Nancy reveals that in spite of her still being guided by 'rigid principles', she will no longer cling to them if given evidence that they do not apply. She has accepted that she and Godfrey are not going to have any further children: 'When you saw a thing was not meant to be, said Nancy, it was a bounden duty to leave off so much as wishing for it'. Even so, she is willing to support Godfrey in his determination to claim Eppie and bring her back to live at The Red House. Eppie's decision to stay with Silas prevents this; it signals an intuition that the worlds to which she and her father belong are separate. Godfrey's willingness to allow Eppie to stay with Silas thus reflects Nancy's final acceptance of the lot given to her and her husband. Just as she did not become 'the Squire's wife' as she once wanted (she is plain Mrs Cass, childless but content), so she has resisted the temptation of thinking she can change the past by adopting a child. Instead, she recommits herself to Godfrey, a gesture symbolized by Eppie's marriage to Aaron. . . .

This reading of the relation between the two plots of *Silas Marner* not only provides a frame for the examination of the many intricate features of this particular novel but also raises a great many issues relevant to the analysis of women's writing in general. If one is to understand the psychological implications of a text for its author, one must first establish the identity of the character to whom the narrative events are most directly related. This character is not always one of the protagonists of the surface structures. Nancy is a very minor character in Part 1 of the novel but, as I have shown, the events of Part 1 are all directly related to her and to the dilemma confronting her.

In psychological terms, the novel is not composed of two 'plots' of equal value. It tells one story on two different levels of fictional representation. It is about Nancy's relationship with Godfrey, which has been made difficult as a result of an overattachment to her father and a corresponding tendency to suspect the worth of any other man. It tells how Nancy gradually overcomes a self-destructive tendency to indulge in unconscious fears, fantasies, and arbitrary decisions detrimental to the happiness she desires. By working at her relationship with Godfrey, she gradually overcomes those deeply-ingrained tendencies in her character which could so easily have led her into increasing emotional isolation and prevented her from making her peace with Godfrey, as she so evidently wants to do. The novel traces the process Nancy unconsciously goes through before she finally, albeit only tentatively, comes to terms with her situation: she is (and in all likelihood will remain) childless, but she now knows that the 'partner' in her own imagination fully accepts their situation.

NANCY AND GEORGE ELIOT

Although I have endeavoured to show that one can deduce Nancy's central function in the novel only from textual evidence, the basis of my argument supposes that the dilemma facing Nancy must also be relevant to George Eliot. There are, however, few obvious parallels between Nancy and Marian Evans. The fictional character is clearly not the carrier of the author's conscious personality, but the carrier of an aspect of her unconscious personality.... There is no reason why the pivotal character in a novel should resemble the author. But, just as the dream-ego's *behaviour* will always reveal an important aspect of the ego's unconscious personality, so too, in a novel, will the pivotal character's reactions to the dilemma facing him/her reveal an important aspect of its author. Nancy's reactions have much in common with those of George Eliot.

Silas is about forty years old at the beginning of the novel, and Nancy is about forty years old at the end—Eliot's age at the time of writing. We know that the novelist's early life was considerably affected by her relation with her father. When Nancy separates herself sufficiently from her father to set her hopes on Godfrey she is about the same age as Marian Evans was in 1842, when her refusal to go to church led to a violent quarrel with her father. In spite of this, however, he continued to influence her greatly, even after his death. Marian met G.H. Lewes in October 1851: he was still married, even though he was no longer attached to his wife. She knew the indignity of having to keep her affair with him secret—the parallel with Molly is obvious; Nancy, one notes, suffered no less for her 'secret' love for Godfrey. Her instinct to withdraw into herself and to cross-question herself mercilessly was shared by her creator, who was unusually depressed throughout 1860, occasioned at least in part by society's continued refusal to accept her relation with Lewes. In spite of all the love by which she was surrounded, and for all her literary success, she continued to be prey to an astonishing lack of confidence in herself. Dessner and others have drawn attention to a great many parallels between the life and the fiction. There is ample evidence to suggest that the dilemma I have identified as confronting Nancy is comparable to that which faced Eliot in 1860. Its ending represents a tentative resolution to an enormously painful personal experience that 'thrust' itself upon Eliot in 1860. . . .

This conclusion raises one further question, and one must touch on it even though it cannot be satisfactorily resolved. To what extent was Eliot conscious of the nature of the dilemma I have outlined? We can never know, but that Nancy never fully realizes the debt that she, no less than Godfrey, owes to Silas signals that the ending represents but a tentative solution to the problem with which the novel is concerned. Nancy may never again give way to such fears as occasioned her initial withdrawal from life, but her author might. Indeed, one notes that a considerable part of *Felix Holt* is a development of the theme explored in *Silas Marner*, which would suggest that Eliot only very partially integrated the lesson learned by Nancy at the end of her tale about the weaver of Raveloe. One remembers Mrs Transome's bitter remark: 'A woman's love is always freezing into fear. She wants everything, she is secure in nothing [. . .] God was cruel when he made woman.' *Silas Marner* illustrates how a woman who is uncertain of her feminine worth risks falling victim to negative fantasies of her own devising and illustrates the psychological origin of Eliot's own deep-rooted insecurity, succinctly expressed by Nancy's 'longing for what was not given'. It tells how a woman whose love had frozen into fear unconsciously discovered a 'light enough to trusten by' that allowed her to achieve at least a partial escape from her own self-doubts and a partial fulfilment of her desires.

Three Stages of Moral Development

Bernard J. Paris

In this article, Bernard J. Paris describes the three
basic manners in which characters in George Eliot's
novels relate to the world. These three approaches
are egocentric, alienated, and meaningful. Some
characters remain "stuck" in one approach while
others evolve from the self-centeredness of egoism to
a more meaningful and objective understanding of
other people as autonomous individuals who are
equally troubled by life's burdens. Paris applies these
three approaches in particular to the main characters in *Silas Marner*, Godfrey Cass and Silas Marner.
Dr. Bernard J. Paris is the director of the Institute for
Psychological Studies of the Arts at the University of
Florida. Dr. Paris has written several books on the
psychological approach to literature, including *A
Psychological Approach to Fiction; Studies in Thackeray, Stenhal, George Eliot, Dostoevsky, and Conrad*
and *Bargaining with Fate: Psychological Crises and
Conflicts in Shakespeare and His Plays*. This article is
excerpted from Dr. Paris's book, *Experiments in Life:
George Eliot's Quest for Values*.

There are three basic ways, in George Eliot's novels, in
which self relates to the world. It may relate to the world
egoistically (or subjectively), in which case the distinction
between the inward and the outward is obscured; self is seen
as the center of the world and the world as an extension of
self. It may be overwhelmed and threatened with annihila-
tion by the hard reality of the world; it then experiences a
state of disillusionment or disenchantment in which the
world, even the human order, is seen as a totally alien, nonhuman existence and self as dehumanized, as completely

Excerpted from *Experiments in Life: George Eliot's Quest for Values*, by Bernard J.
Paris (Detroit: Wayne State University Press, 1965). Reprinted with permission from
the author.

insignificant or spiritually homeless. Or, retaining its integrity but giving up its egocentricity, it may relate to the world at once meaningfully and objectively, seeing the world as an autonomous existence of which it is a part. . . .

STAGE 1—SELF AND EGO

The egoist is often a gambler: he may engage in actual games of chance, . . . with the confident expectation that he will win; or he may be a worshipper of fortune and live in hope that the realization of his desires or escape from punishment for wrong-doing will somehow be granted to him. Take the case of Godfrey Cass. Because of his secret marriage Godfrey is afraid of being disowned by his father and cut off forever from Nancy Lammeter. He lives in dread of the disclosure of his secret which may come through Dunstan or through his wife. Godfrey often thinks of confession, but he continues to get himself more deeply involved in lies and debts. When a crisis appears imminent, Godfrey flees "to his usual refuge, that of hoping for some unforeseen turn of fortune, some favourable chance which would save him from unpleasant consequences—perhaps even justify his insincerity by manifesting its prudence." "In this point of trusting to some throw of fortune's dice," George Eliot comments, "Godfrey can hardly be called old-fashioned. Favourable Chance is the god of all men who follow their own devices instead of obeying a law they believe in. . . . The evil principle deprecated in that religion is the orderly sequence by which the seed brings forth a crop after its kind."

Events take their natural course: such characters as Godfrey, . . . are eventually victims of the nemesis set in motion by their lawless actions. And because of the connectedness of things, many others must share the consequences of the egoist's random, short-sighted, or deliberately selfish behavior. Since his desires are not chastened by submission to law and his actions are not governed by a true vision of the relations of things, the egoist is truly at the mercy of circumstances, and his desires are more often frustrated than satisfied. . . .

STAGE 2—SELF AND DISILLUSION

Man is innately egoistic; it is natural for the mind initially to view all things as extensions of or as related to self. It is equally natural, however, for experience to make clear to the individual the disparity between self and non-self. The discovery of the otherness in things and people comes in many ways, all of which are painful, though in varying degrees. . . . Silas Marner becomes a dehumanized hermit and miser. The egoist is wakened from his self-indulgent dreams to the harsh reality of life. He is taken out of his private world and enters the world of his fellow men, who are also fellow sufferers. . . .

In Chapter I Silas has everything that makes his life human and meaningful stripped away from him. His trouble springs initially from the too great trust which he placed in his friend, William Dane: "whatever blemishes others might discern in William, to his friend's mind he was faultless." When he is accused of theft, Silas realizes that William has deceived him. He tells his inquisitors: "I am sore stricken; I can say nothing. God will clear me." But the lots declare him guilty, and Silas, whose trust in man has been sorely bruised, now loses his faith in divine justice: he declares that "there is no just God that governs the earth righteously, but a God of lies, that bears witness against the innocent." "Poor Marner went out with that despair in his soul—that shaken trust in God and man, which is little short of madness to a loving nature." The final blow falls upon Silas when Sarah, his betrothed, casts him off and marries William. Silas leaves his native town and emigrates to Raveloe.

In Raveloe Silas lives in almost complete estrangement from society, his only contact with his neighbors being in matters of business. In his new surroundings he is one of "those scattered linen-weavers" who "were to the last regarded as aliens by their rustic neighbours, and usually contracted the eccentric habits which belong to a state of loneliness." In addition to being a stranger, a linen-weaver (whose skill is suspicious), and an odd looking sort of man, he is also an epileptic; and his fits, which made him an object of special respect in Lantern Yard, make him an object of fear and distrust to his new neighbors. His appearance "would have had nothing strange for people of average culture and experience"; he suffers from the narrowness of the superstitious and provincial inhabitants of Raveloe.

But not only is Silas alien to his fellows; his new neighbors and surroundings are entirely alien and unintelligible to him. He lives now in a "strange world" which is a "hopeless riddle" to him. Raveloe is different from Lantern Yard in every way—in appearance, economy, customs, religion; and his experience is like that of the primitive man who has left the territory ruled by the tribal divinities and entered a land of strange gods. Even his own past, disconnected as it is from the present, becomes remote and unreal for him. George Eliot remarks that

> even people whose lives have been made various by learning, sometimes find it hard to keep a fast hold on their habitual views of life, on their faith in the Invisible, nay, on the sense that their past joys and sorrows are a real experience, when they are suddenly transported to a new land, where the beings around them know nothing of their history, and share none of their ideas—where their mother earth shows another lap, and human life has other forms than those on which their souls have been nourished.

Silas' life comes to center around his loom and his money. He becomes dehumanized in his mechanical activity and his hoarding; his life is narrowed and hardened "more and more into a mere pulsation of desire and satisfaction that had no relation to any other being. . . . Strangely Marner's face and figure shrank and bent themselves into a constant mechanical relation to the objects of his life, so that he produced the same sort of impression as a handle or a crooked tube, which has no meaning standing apart" (Chap. II). At the same time, Silas endows his loom and his money with consciousness and they become his companions, responding to his feelings.

Silas Marner is the story not only of Silas' despair and alienation from the human world; it is the story also of his slow rehabilitation and integration into the life of Raveloe. George Eliot reflects, after Silas' money is stolen, that although his life may have appeared withered and shrunken, "in reality it had been an eager life, filled with immediate purpose which fenced him in from the wide, cheerless unknown. . . . But now the fence was broken down—the support was snatched away" (Chap. X). The theft of his money, which brings Silas to the lowest point of desolation, is the turning point in his relations with his fellows:

> Left groping in the darkness, with his prop utterly gone, Silas had inevitably, a sense, though a dull and half-despairing one, that if any help came to him it must come from without; and there was a slight stirring of expectation at the sight of his fellow-men, a faint consciousness of dependence on their goodwill. (Chap. X)

Through Dolly Winthrop and especially through Eppie, whom the loss of his gold has prepared him to welcome and love, Silas comes to partake in the customs and forms of

Raveloe life; he becomes once more a part of the world around him. He even comes to have faith in the goodness of the world. Referring to the incident at Lantern Yard, Dolly Winthrop says: "And if you could but ha' gone on trustening, Master Marner, you wouldn't ha' run away from your fellow-creatures and been so lone." "Ah," Silas replies, "but that 'ud ha' been hard . . . ; it 'ud ha' been hard to trusten then." But now Silas can share Dolly's faith in the divine love: "There's good i' this world—I've a feeling o' that now; and it makes a man feel as there's a good more nor he can see, i' spite o' the trouble and the wickedness" (Chap. XVI). Silas' feelings about the invisible are, we see, the direct product of his experiences with his fellow men. . . .

STAGE 3—SELF AND OBJECTIVITY

When we regard others objectively we see things, including ourselves, from their point of view; we put aside, for the time, the claims of our own ego and imaginatively project ourselves into the interior life of the other person, feeling for him as he feels for himself (or as we feel for ourselves). In January 1875 George Eliot wrote . . . : "I am very fond of that old Greek saying that the best state is that in which every man feels a wrong done to another as if it were done to himself."

The objective approach to reality involves the recognition of moral law which is independent of self and to which the individual must submit himself. An important function of religion, for George Eliot, is to make the individual conscious of a rule of right which is superior to impulse. The very nature of religious assemblies, she wrote, is that they involve "the recognition of a binding belief or spiritual law which is to lift us into willing obedience and save us from the slavery of unregulated passion or impulse." The objective relation of self to reality involves also an awareness of the autonomy of the world and of other people, a vision of the true relations of things, and an acceptance of the inevitable and a striving for the possible. . . .

Through experience, by having the true nature of things painfully impressed upon his consciousness, the egoist frequently comes to adopt the objective point of view. After they have been married and childless for many years, Godfrey, moved by the discovery of Dunstan's body and Silas' money, tells Nancy that Eppie, whom he has been wanting to adopt, is really his own child. Nancy consents to adopt her and Godfrey is confident that his wish will finally be realized: "It seemed an eminently appropriate thing to Godfrey, for reasons that were known only to himself; and by a common fallacy, he imagined the measure would be easy because he had private motives for desiring it." Godfrey, however, encounters determined resistance from Marner and especially from Eppie, and he is made aware of the existence of powerful feelings in others and of the irrevocability of his actions. Nancy remarks that they "can't alter her bringing up and what's come of it." Godfrey replies: "No . . . there's debts we can't pay like money debts, by paying extra for the years that have slipped by. While I've been putting off and putting off, the trees have been growing—it's too late now." Godfrey recognizes now that "I'd no right to expect anything but evil could come of that marriage [his first]—and when I shirked doing a father's part too." Godfrey recognizes now how little right he had to be cross to Nancy because of their childlessness:

> "And I got *you*, Nancy, in spite of all; and yet I've been grumbling and uneasy because I hadn't something else—as if I deserved it."

> "You've never been wanting to me, Godfrey," said Nancy with quiet sincerity. "My only trouble would be gone if you resigned yourself to the lot that's been given us."

> "Well, perhaps it isn't too late to mend a bit there. Though it *is* too late to mend some things, say what they will." (Chap. XX)

Arthur Donnithorne [in *Adam Bede*] undergoes a change of attitude similar to Godfrey's. He learns that the evil consequences of past wrongdoing can be only partially mitigated—and Arthur is ready to undergo any self-sacrifice to lessen the evil. Arthur does much to mitigate the evil for the Poysers and the Bedes, but he can do nothing to make it up to Hetty. At the very end of the novel he says to Adam: "I could never do anything for her, Adam . . . and I'd thought so of the time when I might do something for her. But you told me the truth when you said to me once, 'There's a sort of wrong that can never be made up for'" (Epilogue).

Often the three stages of relation between self and the world which I have been describing are, in the order presented, also stages of intellectual and moral development through which George Eliot's characters go in the process of maturation. "We are all of us," she writes in *Middlemarch*, "born in moral stupidity, taking the world as an udder to feed our supreme selves." Almost all of her major characters experience the second stage in which harsh reality breaks in upon and destroys the illusions (some of them innocent enough) about self and the world which are concomitant with inexperience and with immature or selfish subjectivity. Her characters cannot reach the third and ultimate stage of moral development without going through the trial and sorrow which results from their experience of the world's harshness or indifference. This experience makes clear to them the real relations of things and makes them sharers in the common lot. If it does not drive them back into illusion or into an embittered, defensive egoism, it nurtures in them the vision and sympathy necessary for the highest human fellowship.

CHAPTER 4

Structure and Language

READINGS ON
SILAS MARNER

Blending Realism and Allegory

Jerome Thale

Jerome Thale's essay examines two seemingly contradictory aspects of Eliot's *Silas Marner:* its use of allegory and its use of realism. Thale explains that, as an allegory, the text is a moral tale in which particular characters represent specific religious virtues or values. But, Thale also asserts, the tale is based firmly on a true historical and social system. To contrast these two different aspects of the novel, Thale draws a comparison between Silas Marner and Godfrey Cass. Thale argues that Eliot manages to balance the two different types of literature (allegory and realism) by placing side by side the values and belief systems of the two diverse characters of Silas and Godfrey. Jerome Thale is the author of *The Novels of George Eliot,* from which this selection has been excerpted.

We all remember the story of Silas: how the simple weaver is betrayed, how he comes to the village of Raveloe and lives in isolation for fifteen years, hoarding his money. How his gold is stolen, how he finds a child in the snow, and how she at last is the means of his redemption. We also remember, though less distinctly, that the child is the daughter of the young squire Godfrey Cass by a slatternly wife whom he cannot acknowledge, and that Silas's gold is stolen by Dunstan Cass, Godfrey's worthless brother. And we remember that when, after many years, Godfrey acknowledges his daughter, she rejects him for Silas. The meaning of *Silas Marner* as a moral allegory is obvious enough, and the symbols are the familiar ones of Christianity. Silas hoards the treasure that kills his own spirit, the treasure that moth and rust consume and a thief steals; then he finds and stores up another treasure, the golden-haired Eppie. The gold brings death to Dunstan, but its loss brings life to Silas.

Taken on this level, *Silas Marner* is palatable enough, and its charm is genuine, but such a reading cannot engage us very deeply and does not at all satisfy the facts of the novel. For one thing, almost half of the book is devoted to Godfrey Cass; for another, the manner of the Godfrey story is very different from that of the Silas story—it is realistic where the Silas story is pastoral and fairy-tale-like. . . .

Silas Marner as Allegory

It seems to me that we must take a second look at the Silas story to see what it is about and what kind of story it is. In import and in over-all tone it is clearly some kind of allegory or fairy tale. Although the insistently allegorical import may keep us from thinking of it as a piece of realistic fiction, it is constructed completely within the limits of conventional realism, with careful attention to probability and to verisimilitude of detail. This shows up even in incidental reflections of the times—its treatment of the rise of industrialism, for example, is both accurate and perceptive, and its critique of utilitarianism is a good deal more subtle than the crude attack in *Hard Times* [by Charles Dickens].

We can see this story about a weaver as being in what one might call a central tradition of the nineteenth century, the tradition of the crisis and conversion. . . .

George Eliot was interested in the workings of the soul, and so she tended to see the problem in a way that is familiar to us, if new in her time, to take large issues in terms of psychology. On the surface Silas's experience of crisis and conversion is religious, and one can even take it as a kind of allegory of the intellectual movement of the age. Silas is first seen as a member of a grubby dissenting chapel. His best friend falsely accuses him of theft, the congregation expels him, and he loses his faith and becomes a miser. After fifteen years of isolation he finds Eppie and is redeemed by his love for her. At the end of the novel we see him no longer isolated from the community, but happy, friendly with his neighbors, and a regular churchgoer. Silas's route is like that of the Victorian intellectual—from earnest belief through disbelief to a new, often secular, faith. As psychologist and as student of the new theology, George Eliot saw religion as valid subjectively rather than objectively. For her, our creeds, our notions of God, are true not as facts but as symbols, as expressions of states of mind. Faith is good and disbelief bad, not because a god exists, but because they are symptoms of a healthy and an unhealthy state of consciousness. The novel does not give statements as explicit as this, but that is surely the inference to be made from the action.

Taken in this light, Silas's blasphemy—his statement that he cannot believe in any god but a malevolent one—is important not as a theological proposition but as an indication of some change in his personality, a change resulting from his shattering and disillusioning experience. For when he has lost his trust in his fellow men and in the only institution that seemed to offer him security and give largeness and direction to life, he is impelled to reject that institution and its account of the world. What he has lost is not a creed but a sense of the world.

THE MIRACLE IN *SILAS MARNER*

And a sense of the world is what he regains upon his redemption. To bring this about, George Eliot uses the ordinary device of a fairy tale—a miracle. The situation is splendidly ironic, for the miracle—Eppie's coming—is a purely natural occurrence. Momentarily at least it deceives the myopic Silas (he takes her hair for his lost gold); its effects, however, are like those of a miracle. . . .

Since Silas is a weaver and not a Victorian intellectual, the final resolution of his crisis leaves him believing in God again and going to church on Sunday. But his new religion is really an acceptance of the prevailing local account of the world. It is a symbol of his sense of integration, of his oneness with himself, with nature, and with his fellow men— the reflex of pleasant and harmonious experience, just as his earlier disbelief is the reflex of betrayal and injustice. He has returned not to religion but to a better state of mind. . . .

This, then, is what the Silas Marner plot is about—what kind of a sense of the world we can get from experience and how we come to that sense. It is, to repeat, about attitudes toward the world, states of mind, not ideologies or creeds. Silas's ultimate solution and the process that brings him to it are Wordsworthian [comparable to the beliefs and philosophy of the romantic poet William Wordsworth]. During his period of dryness there are hints of what will redeem him. Seeing a dropsical woman he has a flickering of feeling and offers to treat her with the herbs his mother had taught him about. The incident brings "a sense of unity between his past and present life, which might have been the beginning of his rescue from the insect-like existence into which his nature had shrunk." When his water pot breaks he has enough of the pathetic remnants of piety to save the pieces and set them together in their accustomed place. The actual redemption occurs through Eppie. When he first sees the child, she reminds him of his little sister, and he is taken back to many memories—the Wordsworthian way, joining maturity with the simplicity and purity of childhood. "It stirred fibres that had never been moved in Raveloe—old quiverings of tenderness—old impressions of awe at the presentiment of some Power presiding over his life; for his imagination had not yet extricated itself from the sense of mystery in the child's sudden presence, and had formed no conjectures of ordinary natural means by which the event could have been brought about." As George Eliot has already indicated, the root of Silas's trouble is inability to feel—delight in nature, love for others, satisfaction with himself, interest in the objects of everyday life. His emotional life shrunken and channeled into love of gold, he must at forty begin to learn reverence, piety for nature and for the common details of life. And Eppie is the agent of this—"As the child's mind was growing into knowledge, his mind was growing into memory."

Such is the process that redeems Silas from a meaningless existence. Its issue, as we have seen, is a restoration of love and faith. At the end of Silas's story, we feel that the world which made him happy must be good. Certainly this is a . sense of the world that we should like to accept. But our own experience and observation compel us to acknowledge that the world is not that good. Like Wordsworth's poetry, the Silas story demands certain sanguine assumptions about the world and human experience which we cannot easily make. George Eliot does not ordinarily give such a hopeful view of life; rather, she suggests that there is much suffering, much dullness to be endured. The Silas story, taken by itself, offers us immensely more hope and reassurance than any other of her novels, but it does so less convincingly. The belief in goodness of heart, the belief that nature never did betray, are totally unexamined. It is true that there is some equity in that Silas's suffering is compensated for by his happiness with

Eppie. But this happiness comes about only as the result of chance, or as Silas sees it, a miracle. In an extra-natural account of reality it is possible to accept chance as a symbol, expressive of providence or of beneficent order in the universe. For we allow faith to supplement and sometimes supersede an experiential account of the world. It is of course just this that Silas does. He comes to accept a reassuring view of life, embodied for him in the Church of England; and in this scheme Eppie's coming is not a miracle as he first thought but part of the working of Providence (the miracle is its own evidence for its miraculousness). But the naturalistic presuppositions of the novel, the reduction of everything to the facts of experience, rule out any such providential view of human affairs. Silas is restored and believes, but can those who do not have Silas's good luck see the universe as harmonious and beneficent, see good as conquering evil and dullness? What happens to the simple-minded Silas gives him grounds for trusting, but it seems to offer a critical mind no particular grounds for trusting, believing, or loving.

This may seem to be taking unfair advantage of the novel by applying realistic criteria to an incident which is part of a fairy tale. Certainly the coincidence and the happy ending do not bother us; they are familiar enough in literature. What does bother us is that the coincidence must stand as some sort of proof or justification for Silas's view of a providential and harmonious working of the universe at the same time that the novel works in a realistic framework of strict probability in which coincidence is forbidden as a distortion of reality. Should we say, then, that the use of coincidence is an artistic defect stemming from the expression of a vain hope? . . .

THE REALISM OF *SILAS MARNER*

The rest of George Eliot's work, with its disenchantment, is a relevant argument here. It also is evidence for the seriousness of her concern with the problem of what kind of sense of the world our experience justifies. To resolve the antinomy at which we have arrived and see in what way we must take the Silas story, we must think of it as only one half of a novel, the other half of which is the Godfrey story.

The stories are related in a parallel and complementary way. The fortunes of the two men alternate, and there is a series of pairings in character and situation. Godfrey refuses a blessing and is unhappy, Silas accepts it and is made happy.

Just as Godfrey has two wives, so Silas has two treasures, and each of the two men is a father to Eppie. Godfrey is betrayed by his brother Dunstan, Silas by his friend William Dane. Godfrey is secretly guilty, Silas secretly innocent. Dunstan and the gold are buried together, for the gold is Silas's undoing and the blackmailing brother is Godfrey's. When the gold and Dunstan's body are brought to light it is for Silas's joy and Godfrey's shame. Gold passes from Silas to the Casses, Eppie from the Casses to Silas.

All these parallels and contrasts indicate the care with which the novel as a whole is worked out; more significantly, they point to the fact that the two stories involve the same theme, that Godfrey's story is Silas's transposed into a minor key. Godfrey like Silas is alienated from himself and from society. He endures a period of desolation almost as long as Silas's—fifteen years—not warped and isolated as Silas is, but incapable of happiness, uneasy over his deceit and his failure to acknowledge his daughter. Silas's exile ends when Godfrey's begins, and the transfer of the golden-haired child is symbolic. The general pattern of the two stories is identical, but for Godfrey there is no happy ending.

The point of the thematic parallelism becomes clear when we think of the contrast in tonality between the two stories. Remembering the Silas story we think of the fire on the hearth, the golden-haired girl, the sunny days, the garden, the bashful suitor. Even in his desolation Silas is seen against a pastoral landscape. Compare the introduction of Godfrey:

> It was the once hopeful Godfrey who was standing, with his hands in his side-pockets and his back to the fire, in the dark wainscoted parlour, one late November afternoon. . . . The fading grey light fell dimly on the walls decorated with guns, whips, and foxes' brushes, on coats and hats flung on the chairs, on tankards sending forth a scent of flat ale, and on a half-choked fire, with pipes propped up in the chimney-corners: signs of a domestic life destitute of any hallowing charm, with which the look of gloomy vexation on Godfrey's blond face was in sad accordance.

All through the Godfrey story the atmosphere is dull and oppressive. The story opens with Godfrey deprived of any prospect of happiness by his marriage to a dissipated barmaid, caught unable to replace his father's money which he has given to Dunstan, and threatened with exposure by both his brother and his wife. The story ends with Godfrey absenting himself from Raveloe on the wedding day of the daughter who has rejected him. In the years between there is the guilt and self-reproach over abandoning Eppie and deceiving his wife, there is Nancy and Godfrey's childlessness, and Nancy herself, narrow, barren, just dissatisfied. Even the minor figures in Godfrey's story are unhappy: the old squire is vaguely discontented, indulgent and resentful, a figure of quiet misery. It is a world greyed throughout, given up to "the vague dulness of the grey hours." No one is acutely unhappy as Silas is, but they are people who seem to sense that they are never to have much joy, that their usual happiness is the absence of pain.

THE TWO VISIONS OF *SILAS MARNER* COMBINED

Of course, the difference between the two stories is proper enough since one is a fairy tale and the other a piece done in George Eliot's usual disenchanted realism. But this only describes the difference and does not account for it, does not tell us why the two stories are brought together, what the juxtaposition of two such different views of life means. . . .

George Eliot presents Silas and Godfrey: both of them weak in character and unskillful in battling events, both with unhappiness thrust upon them. Godfrey's story is so faithfully realistic that we have no difficulty in accepting it. And the fairy-tale treatment in the Silas story universalizes what is really individual experience, so that we feel that happiness is really possible, the world tolerable for a great many people, even though we see from Godfrey that it is miserable for some.

In *Silas Marner* the two visions, if not reconciled, are at least each given their due. And the book is seamless and free from conflict because the two visions of life are presented on two different levels so as to acknowledge that they are not directly competing accounts of reality. By putting Silas's story in the form of a fairy tale, so as to transcend that strict logic by which both stories cannot be true, George Eliot disarmed the ordinary criticism of this kind of vision (the criticism that is so devastating when applied to [her novel] *Romola*): by denying its literal validity she tried to preserve its essential truth, and by presenting at the same time the story of Godfrey she gave expression to the other side of the case. Only in *Silas Marner* did she find a way to present the two visions of the world as one artistic piece.

The Narrator's Use of Metaphor

Meri-Jane Rochelson

Meri-Jane Rochelson analyzes the structure of *Silas Marner* with regard to its narrator's use of metaphor as a persuasive technique throughout the novel. She discusses how the narrator's employment of metaphors with regard to light and darkness, local "deities," and even "weaving" is sure and effective in the first half of the book. However, she asserts that the metaphoric descriptions of Eppie in the latter half of the novel are not as successful, possibly revealing the narrator's difficulty in describing the complexity of unfolding events. Meri-Jane Rochelson is an associate professor of English at Florida International University. She teaches courses in Victorian literature and women novelists. She has done extensive research on women in Victorian literature and culture and also on Anglo-Jewish literature and culture.

The strong presence of the narrator in George Eliot's novels and the extensive use of metaphor within their texts are both significant characteristics of Eliot's art, and both have received a great deal of critical attention. For the most part, previous studies have focused on either the narrator alone, or on the imagistic content of metaphors without reference to the narrator. . . .

I have chosen to focus my discussion first on a close reading of a passage of overt narrative commentary in *Silas Marner,* to see how metaphor interacts with other forms of persuasion to create the essential bond when the narrator speaks directly to the reader. Later I will deal with the use of metaphor in the presentation of characters, to see how the narrator employs metaphor—in one case quite effectively, in another less so—to shape the reader's response to persons in

Excerpted from "The Weaver of Raveloe: Metaphor as Narrative Persuasion in *Silas Marner,*" by Meri-Jane Rochelson, *Studies in the Novel,* 1983. Reprinted by permission of the University of North Texas.

the novel. By taking three somewhat different perspectives toward the analysis of metaphor as narrative persuasion in *Silas Marner*, I hope to suggest the range of potential in this approach for adding to our understanding of George Eliot's art.

THE NARRATOR IN CHAPTER 2

A passage early in Chapter 2 illustrates how the narrator of *Silas Marner* uses metaphor to bring the reader into the world of the novel, as she explains to the reader Silas's growing alienation from God. Many critics have commented on the way Eliot frequently shifts the perspective of her narrative, like the changing or refocusing of a lens, and she does so in the following passage early in *Silas Marner*. The narrator begins at a medium distance: "And what could be more unlike that Lantern Yard world than the world in Raveloe?— orchards looking lazy with neglected plenty; the large church in the wide churchyard, which men gazed at lounging at their own doors in service-time; the purple-faced farmers jogging along thc lancs or turning in at the Rainbow; homesteads, where men supped heavily and slept in the light of the evening hearth, and where women seemed to be laying up a stock of linen for the life to come." The narrator describes Raveloe as an objective traveler might, surveying its landscape and inhabitants from sufficiently near to infer its complacent abundance, but at a distance that still prevents intimate acquaintance. The picture is in many ways inviting, but the remote perspective suggests a coolness or aloofness which is, in fact, confirmed in the second sentence: "There were no lips in Raveloe from which a word could fall that would stir Silas Marner's benumbed faith to a sense of pain." The narrator's view moves closer in, to Silas, and we see that his soul remains untouched by the bounty and activity around him.

There has not been much metaphor in this section so far, so that when it does appear—in the reference to a word that might "stir . . . benumbed faith—its effect is the more dramatic. Analogies have appeared in the paragraph to this point: the orchards "look" lazy, and the women only "seem to be" storing linen for the afterlife. These comparisons help assure the reader of the narrator's perceptive eye, and the content of the second is appropriate to the discussion of faith and varieties of belief that make up the subject of the passage. But that they are straightforward analogies, drawing attention through their form to the fact that the narrator is creating them and that the reality they illuminate is quite ordinary reality, makes one feel, too, how strongly the narrator is in control. This feeling that one is being led along by a calm, perceptive, controlled narrator contributes as much to one's sense of the comfort of Raveloe as the actual images themselves. It is thus not only the shift in perspective, but also the shift to metaphor, that accounts for the discomfort produced by the sentence about Silas. His faith does not "seem" numb, it *is* numb, and it must be awakened to pain when it begins to feel. . . .

The movement from one means of explanation to another conveys the earnestness of the narrator's desire to explain, and at the same time suggests that nothing can be explained through only a simple presentation of the data. The narrator then makes clear that the shift in perspective (from Raveloe to Silas, from survey of community to analysis of character) and the shift in rhetoric (from literal speech, to analogy, to metaphor) are still not enough to make the reader understand just what Silas Marner is experiencing. The sentence about Silas's benumbed faith is therefore followed by another shift in perspective: "In the early ages of the world, we know, it was believed that each territory was inhabited and ruled by its own divinities, so that a man could cross the bordering heights and be out of the reach of his native gods, whose presence was confined to the streams and the groves and the hills among which he had lived from his birth. And poor Silas was vaguely conscious of something not unlike the feeling of primitive men, when they fled thus, in fear or in sullenness, from the face of an unpropitious deity."

NARRATOR AS TRUSTED GUIDE

The wider view provides a comparison between Silas's plight and the lives of "primitive men," and results from the same philosophical impulse as the employment of analogy and metaphor. What the narrator suggests is that fullness of understanding can only be approached if one compares the situation at hand to other situations like it. At base is the idea that all things can be related; as readers, we feel the narrator to be someone who sees in the world a unity between the petty details of life and the cosmic beliefs of ancient men, who cannot tell the story of one weaver without joining it to the lives of all people in all time. We also sense the narrator's erudition in the fact that she knows about primitive men and their gods; our faith in her reliability as guide and interpreter increases as we appreciate her wisdom. We are impressed by her compassion in going to such lengths to make sure we understand what she is saying, and we are flattered that this wise, all-seeing narrator assumes "we know," as she does, all about ancient religion.

The brief explanation of local deities is presented as a simple, literal, matter of fact. Having already established her own reliability, the narrator thus places the reader in an attitude of respect toward something he might otherwise have treated with some scorn. He is then prepared to sympathize with Silas in his loss of faith. But in a subtle way this particular analogy also prepares the reader to reject, along with the primitive superstitions, certain forms of Christian belief which Eliot is to supplant in the novel with a religion of human compassion. The images of primitive gods take their place beside the lots-drawing of Lantern Yard in a system of references throughout the novel to superstitious faiths whose foundations may be false but whose believers are sincere.

The comparison between Silas and the early believers is stated explicitly, and as the paragraph ends the narrator reminds us of the more immediate comparison with which it began, the contrast between Raveloe and Lantern Yard: "It seemed to him that the Power he had vainly trusted in among the streets and at the prayer-meetings, was very far away from this land in which he had taken refuge, where men lived in careless abundance, knowing and needing nothing of that trust, which, for him, had been turned to bitterness." All the strands of explanation gradually come together here, in a powerful, simple metaphor. The sense of the whole paragraph is finally epitomized in the last sentence of the passage, an example of the "summary metaphor" that characterizes Eliot's narrator's rhetoric. By its very existence as metaphor, this statement adds something to the narration that could not have been rendered exactly any other way: "The little light he possessed spread its beams so narrowly, that frustrated belief was a curtain broad enough to create for him the blackness of night."

This sentence moves from light to darkness as the chapter so far has moved from the spiritual brightness of Silas's early life to the blankness of his later existence. In the "blackness of night" we have the clearest presentation yet of just how desolate his spiritual state is. With the metaphor, a "curtain" comes down on the bright and active scene of Raveloe life; it is blotted out for the reader just as, for Silas, the benevolent possibilities of that life are made invisible by his disillusionment. It is as if the narrator knows the reader cannot truly understand Silas's plight unless he has all the facts, and through every possible means. If we understand the narrowness of his "light," we will not be too impatient with Silas when frustration removes it completely. And in taking such a well-worn metaphor as the "light of faith" and transforming it into a physical light one may possess—a feeble, useless light, at that—the narrator reveals the pathos of Silas Marner's situation while at the same time suggesting the homely, personal quality of faith. We are led to speculate as to the solace a faith might provide, were its light only wide enough.

To this point I have been concerned with the ways George Eliot uses metaphor in overt narrative commentary, both as part of the process of explanation, and in allying the reader with the narrator in that process. But although a reader's sense of "who the narrator is" may come first through such direct intrusions of the narrator's voice, the values of a narrator in any work are in fact presented all through the narrative, even in sections of free indirect speech, which are intended most closely to reflect the thoughts of characters. In *Silas Marner*, as we have seen, the ability to create metaphors reveals the narrator's generous, farseeing moral nature, and this connection between metaphor-making and character appears, as well, when she narrates her characters' ruminations in free indirect discourse. When Godfrey Cass shrinks from confessing to his father the fact of his secret marriage, the narrator traces his reasoning as follows:

> Why, after all, should he *cut off the hope* of them [favorable chances] by his own act? He had seen the matter *in a wrong light* yesterday. He had been in a rage with Dunstan, and had thought of nothing but a *thorough break-up* of their mutual understanding; but what it would really be wisest for him to do, was to try and *soften* his father's anger against Dunsey, and keep things as nearly as possible in their old condition. If Dunsey did not come back for a few days, . . . *everything might blow over.* (8:119–20, emphasis mine)

Godfrey's desperate rationalization is expressed in a series of metaphors so overworked they are clichés. Developed individually most of these metaphors could be reinfused with their original power; we have already seen what Eliot is able to do with the "light of faith." But piled one upon the other as they are here, these hackneyed phrases indicate only the barrenness of Godfrey's verbal and moral resources, as well as the emptiness of his excuses. By ending the chapter with the feeble phrase, "everything might blow over," the narrator emphasizes the futility of all Godfrey's ill-expressed hopes. If we try to imagine the kinds of metaphors the narrator might use to comment on a situation of such moral complexity, we see the difference in ethos that can be revealed through metaphor. It is significant that when Godfrey finally confesses his guilt, but is prevented from easily "making things right," he expresses his resignation by turning around a cliché: "it *is* too late to mend some things, say what they will." Growth of understanding, for Godfrey, takes the form of seeing the limitations in metaphors made lightly.

For the most part George Eliot's touch is sure. In the narrator of *Silas Marner* she has created a wise, compassionate, earnest guide whom the reader willingly joins and follows. As presented by this narrator, the characters in the novel attain a reality which encourages the reader's concern for their fates. There is one case, however, in which characterization falls short of success, to a large extent because of an inappropriate use of metaphor and symbol. This is what we find in the treatment of Eppie.

Part of the problem stems from the novel's insistence on Eppie as Silas's new treasure, the replacement for his lost gold. She is introduced as an agent in the fairy tale plot, her symbolic function noted by both narrator and characters. In the descriptions of Eppie's childhood, the narrator's attempts to portray infantile reality through her mischievous behavior are overshadowed by Eppie's symbolic presence as the replacement for the gold and the agent of Silas's regeneration. And although the reader may well sympathize with the process Eppie brings about, this sympathetic involvement is won more by the narrator's comments and generalizations than by her actual depiction of Eppie as Silas's child. Since none of the other characters in the novel have such a purely symbolic presentation, the child Eppie stands out as an anomaly.

SOME INCONSISTENCIES IN METAPHORS

Part Two of the novel presents greater difficulties. Eppie, grown to young womanhood, has already helped reintegrate Silas into the human community. She still must serve to effect Godfrey Cass's chastening, but she carries out this function not much differently from the ways in which other, less symbolic, characters perform theirs. Thus, although the identification of Eppie with the gold remains strong (the section begins "sixteen years after Silas Marner had found his new treasure on the hearth"), the reader is also invited to view Eppie as a "rounder" character, with her own emotions, decisions, and individual destiny. The narrator's metaphors, however, interfere with one's acceptance of Eppie in this light.

Specific metaphors, as well as more indirect images, depict Eppie as something of a playful animal. She jokes about Aaron Winthrop, "laughing and frisking," and is shown in affectionate communication with the animals around her home, including "a meek donkey, not scornfully critical of human trivialities," and various dogs and kittens with other human attributes. Personification is used quite effectively in other places by the narrator as in the ironic allegorization of "inquiry" that starts Chapter 10, and the "importunate companion, Anxiety," who appears at its end. But in these cases the more abstract metaphors are appropriate where they appear, and consistent with the ethos of the narrator that has been established. The personifications of domestic animals do not seem to fit in their context, because a conflict exists between the content and rhetoric of these metaphors and the implications inherent in other equally strong images. . . .

What one seems to experience in this part of the narrative is an indirect presentation of Eppie's childlike ethos. The problem, of course, is that Eppie is not a child, but a young woman about to be married. The "playful animal" has another side; Eppie's sexuality is suggested repeatedly in the image of her garden, in the unruliness of her hair, and even in her exuberant behavior. That married life is so strongly symbolized by Eppie's garden suggests that the narrator intends sexual awakening to be seen as part of Eppie's fulfilment. But the childish innocence that may also be meant to show the success of Eppie's upbringing does not fit. The metaphors conveying a childlike view of the world are at war with the notion of Eppie as a woman, and finally they overpower it.

It may be that Eppie's innocence is essential to the happy ending the fairy tale plot requires. But Eliot has trouble with happy endings; they tend to become, in her work, too happy, too conventional. Perhaps it is because she believes, with the narrator of *Silas Marner,* "that life never *can* be thoroughly joyous." Straining for the conventions of peaceful contentment, in the portrait of Eppie the narrator fails to reconcile happiness with the complexity of human fates on which the rest of the novel insists.

The relative failure of Eppie's characterization is, however, only the exception that proves the rule. Looking at metaphor as part of a narrator's rhetoric provides an additional dimension to one's understanding of how meaning is conveyed to the reader of a novel. The extent to which a narrator uses metaphor, as well as when and how he uses it, affects the way a reader responds to him—and thus to the narrative—at each point. In *Silas Marner,* the narrator's use of analogy and metaphor allies the reader with her in the process of explanation; at the same time it reveals her own sense of how difficult any explanation is. The moments at which she chooses to employ metaphor, and the kinds of metaphors she chooses, help so strongly to shape one's views of characters and events that at least once the narrator's metaphors produce a response in conflict with what the author seems to have desired.

In *Silas Marner* the use of analogy in narration also has a strong thematic appropriateness. Silas is the "weaver of Raveloe" in more than the literal sense; his misfortune unites his neighbors to him in sympathy just as Eppie reawakens his own sense of ties to the community. The raveled threads of the village are woven into a fabric as Silas and his neighbors each come to see how, despite their first feelings of strangeness from each other, they are in fact mutually connected. By using analogy and metaphor as her predominant means of explanation, the narrator allows the reader similarly to see relationships among apparently disparate phenomena. The theme of universal interconnectedness, which in some way underlies all Eliot's novels, is thus presented through the method of narration, itself, based in the idea that things can best be understood when viewed "in the light of" each other.

CHRONOLOGY

1819

Queen Victoria is born; Mary Anne Evans is born; Walter Scott publishes *Ivanhoe*.

1820

Evans family moves to Griff House in the Midlands, Mary Anne's home until she is twenty-one.

1836

Mary Anne Evans's mother dies.

1837

Coronation of Queen Victoria; Victoria marries Prince Albert; Nathaniel Hawthorne publishes *Twice Told Tales*; Mary Anne's sister Chrissey marries; Mary Anne changes the spelling of her name to Mary Ann.

1841

Evans and her father move to Coventry; Mary Ann befriends Cara and Charles Bray.

1842

Mary Ann rejects Christianity as practiced by Church of England, which enrages her father and causes a temporary breach in their relationship.

1845

Irish potato famine.

1846

Mexican-American War begins; Mary Ann translates and publishes Strauss's *Life of Jesus*.

1847

Emily Brontë publishes *Wuthering Heights*; Charlotte Brontë publishes *Jane Eyre;* William Makepeace Thackeray publishes *Vanity Fair.*

1848

War between United States and Mexico ends.

1849

Mary Ann's father, Robert Evans, dies; she travels with the Brays to the Continent to recover her health and spirits; she remains in Switzerland when Brays return to England.

1850

Poet William Wordsworth dies; Mary Ann returns to England and stays some months with family and friends.

1851

The Great Exhibition opens at Crystal Palace; John Chapman buys the literary and political magazine *Westminster Review;* Mary Ann moves to London and boards with Chapman's family; Mary Ann changes spelling of name to Marian.

1852

Marian Evans begins to work as anonymous editor for Chapman's *Westminster Review;* Marian meets George Henry Lewes.

1853

Crimean War between England and Russia begins; Marian moves to new lodgings in London, helps Lewes correct the proofs for his book on Comte, and tells Chapman she wants to give up editing.

1854

Henry David Thoreau publishes *Walden;* Marian and Lewes begin to live together as man and wife; they travel to the Continent where their relationship is less scandalous; Marian translates Spinoza's *Ethics* and Lewes writes his *Life of Goethe.*

1855

Harriet Martineau publishes her autobiography; Walt Whitman publishes *Leaves of Grass;* Marian and Lewes return to London; Marian writes articles and edits *Westminster Review.*

1856

End of Crimean War; Marian writes "Silly Novels by Lady Novelists" and begins work on the book which will become *Scenes of Clerical Life.*

1857

Blackwood publishes *Scenes of Clerical Life;* the name of George Eliot is first used and Marian Evans's identity is kept strictly secret; Isaac, Eliot's brother, is told of her relationship with Lewes, a situation he never accepts; Eliot begins writing *Adam Bede.*

1858

Scenes of Clerical Life appears in two-volume book form to good reviews; Blackwood suggests publishing *Adam Bede* immediately as unserialized novel.

1859

Charles Darwin publishes *On the Origin of the Species*; *Adam Bede* is published to very good reviews; sister Chrissey dies; Eliot writes short story "The Lifted Veil" and begins *The Mill on the Floss*; Eliot and Lewes travel to Switzerland to visit his sons; Eliot is forced to reveal her identity after someone else is credited with her writing; a breach with Blackwood ensues due to Blackwood's suggestion to publish *The Mill on the Floss* anonymously due to her notoriety; the misunderstanding is resolved.

1860

Eliot finishes *The Mill on the Floss,* which is published to good reviews but is not as successful as *Adam Bede;* Eliot and Lewes travel to Italy, which serves as inspiration for *Romola*; Eliot begins *Silas Marner* in November.

1861

Prince Albert dies; Abraham Lincoln becomes sixteenth American president; American Civil War begins; Dickens publishes *Great Expectations;* Eliot finishes *Silas Marner;* Eliot and Lewes return to Italy to continue her research for *Romola;* Lewes's health, which has been poor, continues to deteriorate.

1862

Eliot finally starts writing *Romola; Romola* is to be serialized in *Cornhill Magazine,* which outbid Blackwood for publication rights.

1863

Eliot finishes *Romola,* which is well received by critics; sales of the three-volume book are flat.

1864

Garibaldi visits England; Eliot writes short story "Brother

Jacob"; Eliot and Lewes travel to Italy; both are in poor health.

1865

American Civil War ends; Lewis Carroll publishes *Alice in Wonderland*; Eliot begins writing both the verse drama *The Spanish Gypsy* and the novel *Felix Holt;* Eliot approaches Blackwood about publishing *Felix Holt.*

1866

Eliot finishes *Felix Holt* and Blackwood publishes it; Eliot returns to writing *The Spanish Gypsy.*

1868

Eliot finishes *The Spanish Gypsy* published by Blackwood to polite reviews.

1869

Eliot begins *Middlemarch;* Eliot and Lewes travel to Italy; they meet John Cross, who will become their financial adviser and later Eliot's husband.

1870

Charles Dickens dies.

1871

Eliot fears she has "too much material" for one novel; Blackwood agrees to publish *Middlemarch* in eight parts at two-month intervals; the novel appears between December 1871 and December 1872.

1873

Eliot begins work on *Daniel Deronda;* Eliot and Lewes travel to France.

1874

Illness continues to plague both Lewes and Eliot; Thomas Hardy publishes *Far from the Madding Crowd.*

1876

Queen Victoria crowned empress of India; *Daniel Deronda* is published; Eliot and Lewes travel to Switzerland but ill health prevents them from going to Italy; Eliot and Lewes buy a country home in England.

1878

Eliot begins *Impressions of Theophrastus Such,* a collection of short essays and character sketches; Lewes dies November 30.

1879

Eliot's publisher, John Blackwood, dies.

1880

Eliot marries John Cross on May 6; Eliot dies on December 22.

1885

John Cross publishes his biography of Eliot.

FOR FURTHER RESEARCH

WORKS BY GEORGE ELIOT

Scenes of Clerical Life (1857)

Adam Bede (1859)

"The Lifted Veil" (short story) (1859)

The Mill on the Floss (1860)

Silas Marner (1861)

Romola (1862–1863)

"Brother Jacob" (short story) (1864)

Felix Holt, the Radical (1866)

"The Spanish Gypsy" (a poem) (1868)

Middlemarch (1871–1872)

Legend of Jubal and other poems (1874)

Daniel Deronda (1876)

Impressions of Theophrastus Such (essay collection) (1879)

These works are accessible in Penguin editions and other common paperback imprints. For informative and well-written introductions to George Eliot's writings, Penguin and Oxford University Press imprints are especially helpful.

EDITIONS OF *SILAS MARNER*

George Eliot, *Silas Marner.* Ed. Anne Smith. Boston: Tuttle, 1993.

———, *Silas Marner: The Weaver of Raveloe.* Ed. Terence Cave. New York: Oxford University Press, 1998.

———, *Silas Marner.* Ed. David Carroll. New York: Viking Penguin, 1997.

———, *Silas Marner.* New York: NAL/Dutton, 1997.

———, *Silas Marner.* Lincolnwood: NTC/Contemporary Publishing, 1998.

———, *Silas Marner.* New York: Bantam, 1981.

BOOKS ABOUT GEORGE ELIOT AND HER WORKS

Walter Allen, *George Eliot.* New York: Macmillan, 1964.

Henry Alley, *The Quest for Anonymity: The Novels of George Eliot.* Newark: University of Delaware Press, 1997.

Rosemary Ashton, *George Eliot: A Life.* London: Penguin, 1997.

Rosemarie Bodenheimer, *The Real Life of Mary Ann Evans: George Eliot, Her Letters and Fiction.* Ithaca, NY: Cornell University Press, 1994.

Oscar Browning, *Life of George Eliot.* London: W. Scott, 1890.

J.W. Cross, *George Eliot's Life as Related in Her Letters and Journals.* 3 vols. New York: Harper and Bros., 1885.

Gordon S. Haight, ed., *The George Eliot Letters.* 9 vols. New Haven, CT: Yale University Press, 1954–1974.

Barbara Hardy, *The Novels of George Eliot.* London: Athlone, 1959.

Margaret Harris and Judith Johnston, eds., *The Journals of George Eliot.* Cambridge, England: Cambridge University Press, 1998.

Peggy Fitzhugh Johnstone, *The Transformation of Rage: Mourning and Creativity in George Eliot's Fiction.* New York: New York University Press, 1994.

Frederick R. Karl, *George Eliot, Voice of a Century: A Biography.* New York: Norton, 1995.

U.C. Knoepflmacher, *George Eliot's Early Novels.* Berkeley and Los Angeles: University of California Press, 1968.

Ruby V. Redinger, *George Eliot: The Emergent Self.* New York: Knopf, 1975.

Jerome Thale, *The Novels of George Eliot.* New York: Columbia University Press, 1959.

Jenny Unglow, *George Eliot.* New York: Pantheon, 1987.

ABOUT ELIOT'S TIMES

Sarah Freeman, *Mutton and Oysters: Food, Cooking, and Eating in Victorian Times*. London: Gollancz, 1989.

Pamela Horn, *Labouring Life in the Victorian Countryside*. Gloucester: Sutton, 1987.

Clark Kitson, *The Making of Victorian England*. New York: Atheneum, 1982.

Daniel Pool, *What Jane Austen Knew and Charles Dickens Ate: From Fox Hunting to Whist—the Facts of Daily Life in Nineteenth-Century England*. New York: Simon and Schuster, 1993.

E.L. Woodward, *The Age of Reform, 1815–1870*. Oxford: Clarendon, 1949.

G.M. Young, ed. *Victorian England: Portrait of an Age*. Garden City, NY: Doubleday, 1954.

ORGANIZATIONS TO CONTACT

The Victorian Society in America
219 South Sixth Street
Philadelphia, PA 19106
phone: (215) 627-4252
fax: (215) 627-7221
e-mail: vicsoc@libertynet.org
website: http://www.libertynet.org/vicsoc

The George Eliot Fellowship
71 Stepping Stones Road
Coventry CV5 8JT UK
phone: (01144) 1203 592231

INDEX